Paul's War
Slovakia, 1938 – 1945

OTHER PUBLICATIONS BY PAUL A. STRASSMANN:

Information Payoff The Transformation of Work in the Electronic Age – 1985
The Business Value of Computers – 1990
The Politics of Information Management – 1994
Irreverent Dictionary of Information Politics – 1995
The Squandered Computer – 1997
Information Productivity – 1999
 Information Productivity Indicators of U.S. Industrial Corporations – 2000
Revenues and Profits of Global Information Technology Suppliers – 2000
Governance of Information Management Principles & Concepts – 2000
Assessment of Productivity, Technology and Knowledge Capital – 2000
The Digital Economy and Information Technology – 2001
The Economics of Knowledge Capital: Analysis of European Firms – 2001
Defining and Measuring Information Productivity – 2004
Demographics of the U.S. Information Economy – 2004
The Economics of Outsourcing in the Information Economy – 2004

Paul's War
Slovakia, 1938 – 1945

Paul A. Strassmann

The Information Econonomics Press
NEW CANAAN, CONNECTICUT
2006

Published by the Information Economics Press
P.O.Box 264
New Canaan, Connecticut 06840-0264
Fax: 203-966-5506
E-mail: publisher@infoeconomics.com
Design and composition: David G. Shaw, Belm Design

Produced in the United States of America

Strassmann, Paul A.
Paul's War
1. Biography; 920;   2. History of Eastern Europe; 947
Version 1.0 – February 2006
Library of Congress Control Number: 2006900809

ISBN 096204136X

Contents

Pictures

To The Murdered, Unavenged:

FILIP STRASSMANN, GRANDFATHER

ANNA STRASSMANN, GRANDMOTHER

ALEXANDER WEINER, GRANDFATHER

ADOLF STRASSMANN, FATHER

FRANZI STRASSMANN, MOTHER

SAMUEL ALTMAN, UNCLE

PAVLA ALTMAN, AUNT

ALICA ALTMAN, COUSIN

IRMA FLACK, AUNT

JOZEF FLACK, COUSIN

ALEXANDER SCHALK, UNCLE

ERNA SCHALK, AUNT

KAROL SCHALK, COUSIN

ALZBETA SCHALK, COUSIN, AND CHILD

EUGEN WEINER, UNCLE

Introduction

As this is written there are already seventeen second, third and fourth-generation descendants of my parents Adolf and Frances Strassmann, who were murdered in 1945. The prospects of the first fifth-generation descendant are not too distant.

One of the grandchildren called to listen to my stories for a school term paper. It occurred to me that there may be others who may have a similar curiosity about the experiences of a teenager who lived through the Second World War from the age of nine to sixteen.

So, here are a boy's recollections, divided into three parts. Part I, *Paul's Story*, covers my personal war experiences. Part II, *Family*, gives the background that influenced development in the youth. Part III, *Slovakia*, describes the setting for the tragedies that would be shaping my life until I left for America.

New Canaan, Connecticut, February 2006

Part I
Paul's Story

Joining Partizans

Whaen the Soviet army started rolling westward after the decisive defeat of the Germans in Stalingrad in February 1943 it was becoming clear with every succeeding month that it was only a question of time and when the German regime would be defeated. Preparations for what everybody called "The End" started in Slovakia early in 1944.

1. Slovakia: Carpathian Mountains Divide the Plains in Poland from the Plain in Hungary. Trenčin is at the Western Mountain Pass Before the Valley Opens

The hitherto dormant anti-Nazi resistance movements began to organize in order to accelerate the transition to eventual liberation.

CIRCUMSTANCES

My father understood that the relative tranquility of our impoverished and restricted circumstances would come to an end as soon as German rules would take over from the order arranged by the Slovak collaborators. My father realized that when the war front would be approaching the Nazis would get rid of as many Jews as possible to eliminate any potential witnesses. The Hlinka Guard would make sure that happened to safeguard the owners of properties expropriated from the Jews. It was said that dead men couldn't ask for justice or restitution of stolen property. Therefore it was probable that we would be eliminated regardless of whether we possessed recently issued papers. What offered protection to us while the initial deportations that took place in 1942 and had resulted in the elimination of most Jews would not hold up anymore. The chances of becoming a casualty were present anyway regardless of being a Jew. The entire civilian population would be taking heavy losses in case my hometown of Trenčín became a defended bastion as it had been for centuries.

I had no idea what Father was planning for the transition to liberation. I could not be trusted to receive such secrets although I later found out there were not many. Much of the energy in those times was spent trying to remain as inconspicuous as possible. Years later my sister shared identical sentiments with me. She never understood what the various approaches to salvation were that we were expected to handle. I guess that was so because there were not that many options. Ever since our family discovered that she served as a courier for illegal activities she was emphatically prohibited from ever engaging in anything that could compromise the safety of the entire family. All the family's plans on what to do as liberation approached were in my father's head. Without his decision, nothing could happen.

Father was a reserve officer of the Czechoslovak army with the rank of major. He was in uniform when the country mobilized at the time of the Munich betrayal. Czechoslovakia's capable army fully armed itself as the country became ready to defend itself. I must suppose that Father had always maintained his military contacts. When the planning for the anti-Nazi uprising started in March of 1944 I suspect that he would be warned about any military preparations for liberation. That is only a guess to explain the instant evaporation of all of our contingency plans after the Gestapo suddenly snatched him. He was one of the handfuls of people, mostly suspected uprising conspirators and military officers, who were seized during the night after the Slovak military uprising was launched on August 28, 1944.

CONTINGENCY PLAN

Father must have known through his contacts with the army that a mutiny would be taking place although he could only guess when that would occur. Nevertheless, late in the third week of August he decided to proceed with an exercise to try out one of our contingency plans. Father anticipated the uprising to break out any moment. Pervasive rumors about isolated small-scale attacks by the partizans on Slovak Nazis were the talk of the day.

The exercise for how to escape Germans required removal to one of the designated villages in the surrounding mountains, Selec. Afterwards we would disperse the family to several peasant homes. After that we would just hunker down, put on inconspicuous clothing, and try to blend in with the local population. We remained in that condition for three days, which was about three days before the uprising started. This escape exercise turned out to be a failure. First, we were noticed as we arrived in daylight in an uncovered truck marked as belonging to my father's former company. Selec is a typical Slovak village in the mountain where the only road winds through a narrow valley formed by a creek. Any truck climbing up the road would be subjected to the scrutiny of hundreds of suspicious eyes. Second, we were seven people. We were not clad in peasant clothing and therefore could not disperse yet into separate cottages. Except for a former army associate of my father's there were no other takers ready to take us in. Lastly, having everyone stay together as a group and to sleep in the same hayloft not only was unpleasant but also led to noisy friction. Compounding the problem was the presence, in the same hayloft, of two hiding Russians who claimed to be escaped prisoners of war. They did not care to have a large Jewish family complicate their refuge.

Meanwhile, several people in Trenčín were wondering where my very well informed father was. His absence would be a sign that trouble was imminent. In the absence of further military developments and with the blown identity in Selec, Father decided for everyone to return home. He must have received the identical assurances as others had that the Slovak army would do everything to avoid a conflict with Germans until the Soviets were ready to start their attack, which had stalled meanwhile in the Polish plains. Because of the many obligations my father had in Trenčín as well as the dependency of my grandparents, we returned from the mountain village, I think, on the 24th or the 25th of August on the identical truck as the one in which we arrived. This is how we used up our first escape option.

THE DISASTER

Three nights later the Gestapo took my father away. I was, by happenstance, sleeping that time at the house of a close friend. This was not planned except that I would be staying too close to the time of the curfew, which started at nine o'clock. I don't remember exactly why but my mother decided I should not come home that night. In the morning, my father and grandfather Weiner were gone. The Gestapo also inquired about my whereabouts.

My mother went into hiding together with the Kubičeks, the closest friends of the family. The hideout was in a house located in a small walled garden practically in the center of the town. It was a few paces from where my parents had their wedding reception twenty years before. I never saw or received any messages from her again. Her hiding place was betrayed in a few weeks and she was seized. According to the International Red Cross, the only records available about Frantiska/Franzi Strassmann is an entry that on the 20th of November, 1944 she was deported from the concentration camp in Sered, Slovakia from where she was transported to the concentration camp in Ravensbruck, Germany as prisoner #84985, category "political-Jewish." Mother died there of typhus fever late in the spring of 1945.

The Choices

To activate the urban hiding contingency plan set up for me and for my sister, I received a message to hurry to the house of someone who had been my father's trusted employee for many years. My sister had previously received proper identification papers and left Trenčín to find a way of disappearing in the Bratislava metropolis. That worked for only a short time until a passerby recognized her and informed the police. She was immediately transported to the concentration camp in Ravensbruck where she briefly met with Mother under indescribable circumstances. I did not see or hear about her fate until she suddenly appeared in Trenčín early in June 1945 as an emaciated slave labor camp survivor.

After I arrived in my prescribed hideout, the following day the Gestapo announced that reprisals would be taken against all supporters of the uprising. Soldiers who did not report by that evening back to army quarters for disarming would be designated as deserters and shot. The local Gestapo command also posted notices all over the town announcing that if they found any partizans, army deserters or Jews hidden in any house everyone in the sheltering family would be executed. When the posters announcing such measures appeared, the wife of my father's trusted employee, in whose house I was hiding in the attic, demanded that during daytime, when the searches were expected to take place, I would have to leave and hide in the bushes growing on the banks of the nearby river Váh.

I remained hidden in the attic for two nights. Early each morning the wife could not get me out of the house fast enough. She pressed into my hand a sandwich and two peaches and let me out through a hole in the back fence of their garden. It was at sunrise when I snuck out through the surrounding fields dressed only in shorts, a cotton belt, a T-shirt, socks and sandals. Retracing back alleys in familiar neighborhoods I ambled to the river and hid in thick bushes that at night used to be places for lovers. I sat there for a couple of hours contemplating my fate. I did not like the situation I was in.

On my second day, I realized that my only option was to sit around and to return after sundown to face an increasingly hostile wife of an obviously hen-pecked husband. By this time I had already acquired my lifelong abhorrence for any situation where I had only one choice of what to do, especially if such a choice would be extremely risky. Returning to the hideout on the second day seemed to me an unacceptable dead end.

By ten in the morning, I heard short bursts of machine gun fire coming from the direction of the Inovec mountain about twenty miles southeast from where I was sitting. Whether it was out of desperation, the awful smell of the proximate sewer that was dumping offal into the river nearby, or cool and rational calculation about my odds of survival, I still do not know to this day, but I made the decision not to return to the hiding place. With nothing more than an instinctive reaction I concluded, with a sense of instant relief, that rather than keep hiding I would go to where the war was being fought and become a hero.

ESCAPE

At the time, I was still sitting on the western bank of the river Váh, a short distance from the only passenger bridge that crossed it. I could see a procession of military vehicles moving back and forth across the bridge. I was sure that sentries would be posted to block my passage. Across the river was the town of Trenčín where I would be instantly recognized if I swam across. The only choice left was to tie up my belongings with my belt around my head, grab a large tree branch for cover and plunge into the river that was flowing southward.

It was early September and the river was at its lowest levels, exposing many sharp rocks and rapids that could rip the skin and result in deep gashes. Luckily, my exclusion, since 1940, from the comforts of the local swimming pool now became useful. I had mastered the skill of floating at the speed of the current down the river as sporting adventure. The drifting took about one hour. It got me safely out of the range of any observers and into a region where there were only small villages. It was a refreshing swim, and it took my mind off what could be happening to my family.

When I emerged from the river, the scenery was serene and peaceful. Peasants were working their plots. As long as I gave them the familiar greeting "God be with you," I got friendly, even if quizzical, smiles in return. It took then another four hours to walk to the village of Selec, the location of my family's first aborted hiding place. Father's contingency-testing exercise turned out to be a blessing because I knew where to go next.

Everything I had learned over the years on about how to blend into the landscape came to me easily. The rules were simple: Never walk on a road; seek a walkway on the cow-paths behind the village barns; do not talk to strangers; do not give your name to anyone; never offer explanations even if asked; even if hungry do not pick somebody's fruit and certainly do not steal; always drink plenty of water from a creek but only if it comes directly from a mountainside; if pressed, act stupid and confused.

When I arrived at the farmhouse where we had been hidden only a few days ago I was told that the surrounding hills were filling up with army deserters. Staying in the village would be too dangerous. I was given peasant pants as well as a cloth jacket and told to start climbing the mountain Inovec to the cottage of a gamekeeper who would surely help me out. At nightfall I finally made it to the cottage where I was welcomed. The gamekeeper knew my father from the military and held him in high regard. Finally I got my first good night's sleep in a hayrick. That is a loosely constructed shelter for storing hay to feed livestock during winter months. In the morning I received a thick slab of bacon, bread and prunes and was told to get lost in the woods for the day because the forest would be crawling with armed Hlinka Guards seeking deserters. My spirits were up because I could hear occasional rifle fire not too far away.

SEEKING PARTIZANS

At noontime, I came across a band of uniformed and lightly armed Slovak army soldiers who were relaxing near a creek. They were headed to Central Slovakia where a liberated Czechoslovak government had been just formed. I begged them to take me along. That resulted in a good-natured laugh because I would be unfit to be of any military use. As a consolation prize they gave me a hand grenade on the condition that I would vanish as quickly as possible.

At this point it is important to explain how one would use a Slovak hand grenade. It was a black cylinder. One could use it as a concussion grenade, as a booby trap, or, when a metal collar was slipped on it, as a fragmentation explosive. Wound around the cylinder was a strip of spring steel. The grenade exploded when the coiled strip of steel was unwound. Depending on how many of the five layers of the strip were uncoiled, one could control the time between removal of the firing pin and the explosion. When only one turn of steel was left, the grenade would go off exactly in one second. Starting with four windings made it possible to throw the grenade into an open door and still get away. This was all explained to me in a minute. Luckily, I never had the courage to rely on tossing such a confusing grenade without further practice, which never came.

Later on when the supply of these contraptions became plentiful, I was advised to always keep an extra grenade in my satchel in case I get wounded. The grisly humor about that was that if the satchel was properly set up as an easily triggered pillow one would not suffer a headache. This advice was accompanied by an admonition that partizans would never be in the position to take care of their wounded. In partizan warfare, captured prisoners, on either side, were kept alive only for torture.

Thus armed and with a growing confidence in my military capabilities I started walking on a steep path in the direction of where I believe the shots were coming from. When I saw some deer galloping nearby, I took that as a warning and jumped behind a tree. Down the path was coming a tall man with a weapon slung on his shoulder. He carried what I recognized as a Bren gun, which was a favorite of WWII infantry. The man was walking in a most careless manner. I jumped out from behind the tree, with my hand grenade outstretched, and asked him to put the gun down. It was John Kartal, a Jewish man of uncertain means and known in the town as a person of inflated pretensions. He was now on his way to the uprising where he hoped to resume his reserve rank as an officer. It appears that on the first morning of the uprising the doors to the local armory were opened for anyone to take what he or she wished. Kartal just walked out with the best ordnance he could carry. Kartal cursed when I told him he was walking in the wrong direction. We shared my bacon and decided that we would now march together to make war as long as I would relieve him from carrying a heavy satchel in which he carried ammunition clips for the machine gun.

Finding Partizans

By the end of the day, we finally made it to the edge of the forest near the village of Mnichova Lehota. Below us was a highway next to train tracks. John set up the machine gun and asked me to go down to the roadway to check out the situation. In a short while, a small pickup truck pulled up and stopped. Suddenly, out of the woods came seven scraggly figures and headed for the truck. At the head of this group was a little man, with a left arm stump where there used to be an elbow. The man had a cap with a red star emblem. That's how I met my future leader, Batko, also known as "Screw your mother Batko" (sounds better in Russian) because he used that expression to punctuate every few sentences.

I waved Kartal to come out. He immediately informed everyone that he wished to be transported to the commanding headquarters where he expected to assume his rightful position as a Slovak officer. Batko and his band thought this was a joke, but Kartal had the light machine gun they coveted. So, Kartal and I got loaded on the truck and we zoomed about fifteen miles back to a small hamlet, Zavada, on a highway already patrolled by armed German vehicles. Such practice reflected a pattern that would be set for what was to follow. Batko's approach was either utter disregard for operational safety or a boastful demonstration of reckless courage.

So far as I was concerned, I was now euphorically happy. I was in the company of armed men who were looking for ways to kill Germans and Hlinka Guards. And so my partizan life began.

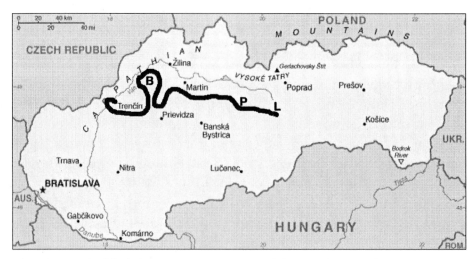

2. Paul's March (black line): B=Base Camps while Attacking Railroad, P=Prašiva, L=Liberation Crossing

The Miners

This partizan squad I first encountered was returning from cutting the tracks on the feeder rail leading from Trenčín to the town of Banovce. Everyone was in great spirits.

The number two man on the partizan squad that accepted me was identified as "Tato," which is a Slovak diminutive for "father." He was a grey-haired old communist and a machinist by trade. He talked rarely, but when he did everybody listened, including his son Michael. Tato was reputed to have served in the Spanish Civil war but nobody could be sure of that except that he often argued with Batko's aggressive ideas on how to proceed without alienating the local population. Tato took Kartal's machine gun and set it up on top of the driver's cab to make us combat ready as we raced down an empty highway where we could have encountered German motorized patrols any time.

I took an immediate liking to such conduct and also loved the spirit of everyone in the band that was boisterously pugnacious. Our team included "Milos," an athletic engineering student from Moravia. Then there was "Ivanko," who claimed to have escaped from a German concentration camp but was always suspected by our political commissar as a turncoat looking to escape his fate when the war ended. "Liška" (little fox) was a local farmer who had problems with a landlord and his wife. Joining partizans seemed to offer a reprieve from all his troubles. Little did he know. Although a little guy, he ended up carrying the Bren gun after we lost Tato.

Batko spent most of his time with the red-haired "Ivanov," who turned out to be a recently parachuted Soviet radio operator as well as the commissar assigned to watch us. Ivanov turned out to be a decent and quiet chap, who did not go on the raids with us but took care of all sorts of procedural matters and what appeared to be an enormous amount of paperwork requested from various commands.

Batko had been parachuted a month before by the partizan command from Kiev. He was a member of a handpicked group of special forces whose sole purpose was to intercept traffic on the main railroad line from Bratislava to Žilina. Batko had been with a partizan unit somewhere in Byelorussia that was originally formed by soldiers who did not surrender when the Germans advanced towards Moscow. The bypassed soldiers avoided getting taken as German prisoners of war by forming partizan units.

Batko was a former professional soldier. As I understood it, when the Soviets liberated territories where there were still some surviving partizans, these highly experienced and tough fighters were immediately redeployed ahead of the advancing Soviets and assigned to high-risk missions. After the war, I found out that any Soviet soldier who had survived either as a prisoner of war or as a partizan was sentenced to hard labor in the Arctic North as someone who could never be trusted by the Communist Party.

Induction

When we finally zoomed into a small hamlet where the partizan brigade command was located, Kartal (less the machine gun) was waved off. Meanwhile, Batko somehow took a liking to me, even though I did not understand a word of what he was saying, because I claimed that I knew all of the mountain trails around Trenčín. This was only partially true. I would learn quickly that brashness and denial of fear could compensate for lots of deficiencies that included my young age of fifteen as well as having never actually fired a gun.

After an obligatory drink of gut-searing home-brew *slivovic* (plum) brandy I was inducted into what was known by the command as "Batko's Miners." The designation of "miners" applied to mine-laying suicidal maniacs. My position was one that involved serving as *rozvedka* (reconnaissance), which in plain English meant walking a hundred yards ahead of the squad and attracting unwelcome situations.

Only Batko had a fully automatic weapon (a Russian PPS with a round magazine containing 72 rounds). I was issued a gendarme's carbine with 128 eight-millimeter rounds after two days of winning everybody's confidence. Into the butt of this highly reliable Mauser-style bolt-action rifle with the capacity of five rounds I carved the name *Pomsta*, which signifies "vengeance" in Slovak. A quarter of my rounds were tracer bullets because we were expected to shoot, if necessary, mostly while it was dark or foggy.

The rest of the squad had miscellaneous hand weapons, including WWI six-shooters as well as standard-issue Slovak army rifles, plus plenty of hand grenades. At the beginning we also carried a Russian 14.5-millimeter antivehicle bolt-action rifle with a fifty-inch barrel. It took two men to carry it, which was inconvenient during our cross-country marches, and so we left it at the headquarters. Our principal objective remained to transport satchels of ten-kilogram steel boxes, each containing TNT explosives as well as a limited supply of blasting caps and yards of ignition cord.

LIFE

During September and for most of October, we had plenty of food. We ate mostly spiced pork stew with beans, cabbage and potatoes. When back at the base we received rations of alcohol, cigarettes and excellent peasant bread. I always traded cigarettes for bread. The food was either bought or sequestered from local peasants. Later, when we were driven out of the villages the rations shrank, especially during the long marches in snow. Even then starving men were still willing to exchange bread for cigarettes, which led to my lifetime aversion to smoking.

On Saturday everybody got a shave. My "beard" was viewed with derision until Batko ruled that since I would probably be killed anyway, I might as well be presentable. When Batko found out that Milos had "never been with a woman," the entire squad chipped in to pay a fee to a more-than-willing local widow while all of us were standing on sentry duty to make sure that none of the relatives interfered. I was offered the same privileges except I was too scared, and, besides I was unable to hold my food. My intestines were full of little white worms I must have picked up from some of the pork I ate early in September.

Otherwise, I remember the period until the end of October 1944 as reasonably happy and sufficiently busy to take my mind off the fate of my family. The days were warm although the nights got increasingly cold until frost and snow arrived in the first week of November and continued until liberation in one of the most severe winters in recent history. When deep snow settled along the mountaintops and in the deep valleys, we could walk only on paths that were inaccessible to German patrols. After snow blanketed the mountains our losses came not from bullets but from exposure to the ever-present numbing frost.

RULES OF ENGAGEMENT

Belonging to the mining squad surely saved my life. We were under orders to stay out of villages, to relocate our campsite every few days, to spend most of the time in marches moving from one attack position to another, to never carry our wounded, to avoid firefights, to run when confronted by any force, never to steal food from the peasants and to always pay cash for services provided by the locals. We always had more than enough Slovak State crowns. The rules dictated that we sleep in hayricks instead of enjoying the greater comfort of the farmhouses, to arrive at points for launching an attack at sunset and to execute missions during nights if at all possible.

I was surprised by the amount of paperwork that was filled out to keep track of what we were doing. Every time our group showed up at another partizan base or when the line of higher command changed (which was often), there was a list to be prepared identifying who we were and where we came from. As I understood it, this was a requirement imposed by the newly formed regular Czechoslovak army who believed that only through proper bookkeeping could we claim to be a properly organized force. Our commissar, Ivanov, had to sign off for every listing. Payroll was the alleged purpose of such tallies. Indeed, we got paid occasionally in Slovak currency. Tato grumbled about such bureaucracy because it would be our death warrant if anyone was captured and one of the lists would be in the hands of our captors, which was quite likely. Batko made it clear, though (with profuse cursing), that all this record-keeping the was an idiotic drill perpetrated by regular army officers who were trying to impose order on chaos even though deliberate disorder would have been the best way for maintaining security.

INTO ACTION

When I met Batko, he was just coming from a sortie that had to be aborted because his people were not familiar with the Trenčín territory. My escape from Trenčín and the exaggerated hand grenade story of how I hijacked a Bren gun received a favorable reception. Batko decided that I was just the right sort of a decoy to place ahead of the next raid.

The next attack on the two-track Trenčín-Žilina railroad line was ordered immediately after the squad returned to the brigade headquarters located at the end of a long, winding road in the small settlement. From the standpoint of Soviet military planning this rail line was strategic because it had the capacity for the rapid transfer of troop reinforcements from the south to the north and vice versa while the Soviets kept the Germans guessing as to the main thrust of the fall offensive that everyone expected.

The objective was to find a curve on the railroad where the wheels of the engine would be pressing hard on the inside of the track. The trick was to find just the right moment when the front of the train would set off a fuse that would then trigger the TNT that would break one of the rails. If that was done right, the locomotive would derail and pull the rest of the trains right off the railroad embankment.

My entire military training took perhaps not more than half an hour. A wooden plank was used to explain how to blow a rail track so that it breaks at the right time. I was to follow Batko who carried in his satchel three metal boxes of TNT (2,4,6-trinitrotoluene). The TNT explosive has a wax consistency that is otherwise inert so that it explodes only when set off by a fuse. My job was to pass to Batko three thin copper tubes, each about three inches long. These contained a toxic mercury picrate explosive that would ignite when hit even with a small force. My job would be to follow Batko to the top of the rail embankment and then pass the fuses as well as strips of adhesive surgical tape to that he could attach the fuses to the outside flange of the rail. Other members of the squad would spread out to provide covering fire in case of pursuit or if we were discovered prematurely.

And so began my first mission against the Germans, setting a pattern to be repeated many times in the two months to come.

THE FIRST RAID

The squad walked as close to the destination as was possible, which was near the village of Opatova. We had to avoid detection because the villages were full of informers. By that time the hills surrounding Trenčín were declared as "open fire" territory. The Germans and their henchmen could shoot anybody on sight that wandered through the woods. That's why we kept off roads and even off paths. Sometimes I had to walk in front of the squad because I knew the environment. In addition to my rifle I also had two hand grenades dangling from my belt, leather pouches with ammunition clips and a backpack with some food and the all-important half of a standard army issue tent. The squad alternated in carrying knapsacks with the explosives.

The first night, the moon was shining so we would walk all night and sleep during the day. Progress was slow. The second night, it started raining lightly. It was very dark. Late in the evening we arrived at the edge of the embankment overlooking the two sets of rails. We wrapped ourselves into the tent-halves to keep dry.

There was not much traffic on the rails below us or on the highway that ran parallel to the tracks. A few passenger trains zipped by. Then a freight train could be heard coming from the south. Its slow puffing indicated that it was pulling a heavy load. Batko was pleased because conditions were ideal for our purposes. The freight train could be heard from a good distance thus giving us about nine minutes' time to mine a rail on the northbound track.

We set up two positions. Following a proven tactic, this called for setting up two flanking positions of two men each spread out about a hundred yards. The mine-laying crew, three of us, then proceeded to place the explosives and arm them. The trick was to cause the train to set off the explosion by its own forward wheels. This was accomplished by taping the blasting cap to the rail. When the front wheel of the locomotive squeezed the cap, it would set off the ignition cord burning at a rate of one foot per second, until the other end would ignite a second blasting cap that was inserted inside the box of TNT. It took skill and experience to figure out what was the necessary length of the cord so that it would blow out beneath the heaviest part of the train, which was the engine tender filled with water and coal.

The flat ground separating the edge of the forest from the railroad was freshly plowed and muddy. There were only two walking paths between adjoining fields. We moved into position in a ditch under the rail embankment. We could now hear the train coming closer. The light rain muffled the sound. We had less than five minutes to set up. I climbed to the rails and sat there watching the headlights of the locomotive approaching. Batko removed some of the stone ballast between the railroad ties and placed two boxes of TNT under the rails. These were set up so that at least one would go off by connecting the detonation cords between the rail and the cavity for a detonator in the top of the TNT container.

Batko now asked for the blasting cap to be attached to one end of the ignition cords with the other end taped to the cap on top of the rail. I was carrying the blasting caps in a thick leather pouch, lined with soft cotton padding. In the excitement of passing the caps I did not snap in the pouch lid completely. All of the caps, maybe a dozen, spilled when I jumped up to follow Batko.

Spilling the blasting cap was a terrible mistake because the squad had no way of replacing these extremely scarce detonators even though we had plenty of TNT. With Batko's work done he got off the embankment and started running back towards the edge of the forest. By this time, the lights from the engine illuminated enough of the roadbed so that I could see the slim, four-inch-long copper detonation cylinders and pick them up in a hurry. I shoved them into my pocket, grabbed my rifle and started running. In an unthinking panic, I made a second horrible mistake. I started running where I had descended from the rail embankment that brought me to the edge of the muddy field instead of the firm path between the plowed plots. In the confusion I could not locate the path.

Imagine running for your life in a sticky paste. After about twenty-five meters I knew that it was time to hit the ground because the locomotive was passing the spot where we had placed the explosives, right behind my back. As I fell to the ground, the TNT charges blew up. Pieces of metal whizzed by me and I heard them digging into the mud. Then I saw the entire front of the train slowly roll off the embankment in my direction, just as Batko had predicted. I could hear the shouts of the occupants of the train and the crunching of metal as rear railcars jammed against the wreck that kept piling up across the rails.

I was not hit by the flying scrap but got slightly singed by the hot water that escaped from the steam boiler. I started running again when I heard a shot followed by a whooshing sound. Arching over me was a white light that exploded into a slowly descending bright flame. The Germans on the armed tail of the train were putting up illuminating flares. I hit the mud again. Tracer bullets from a machine gun passed overhead raking the edge of the forest. When the first flare burned out, I started running again. There were always a few moments between flares allowing me a small advance through the mud. Why nobody saw me remains a mystery, except that I was probably indistinguishable from a lump of mud when I hit the ground. The tracer bullets continued to be fired aimlessly all over the terrain and were obviously targeted too high by concentrating on the edge of the forest.

My luck was that on the train they must have had only a single flare-launching weapon that took a few seconds to reload. Whenever they shot up a flare I could hear a pop before the flare started climbing. It took about three seconds for the flare to get lofted and then to open a small parachute that allowed the bright light to descend slowly. Whenever I heard the flare getting launched I just flattened myself against the mud hoping that the machine gunners would not see me. Luckily, the ground was sufficiently mushy that I became smeared with mud so that when I hit the ground the gunners did not see my silhouette.

The guards on the train must have been inexperienced soldiers. They were wasting ammunition by shooting too high to hit anybody. They used incendiary bullets and were firing blindly from too high an angle in bursts that were not at all aimed during the intervals when the flares did not illuminate the field. The soldiers were high up on a flat car that sat on the embankment, so they did not have the right angle to rake the field at a lethal waist-high level.

The entire squad finally reassembled at the edge of the forest. Nobody was injured. Everyone felt heroic about the damage to the entire front end of a freight train that turned out to be carrying soldiers and most likely their equipment as well.[1] Most of the damage was from the derailment of the locomotive and the tender and not from the explosion. It would take only about half a day for the Slovak maintenance engineers to get the tracks cleared, although even that was considered to be a win from a partizan standpoint.

There were other times when we repeated pretty much the same attack drill but did not end up so lucky. In the absence of reliable intelligence about train schedules there was no way of knowing for sure what we were going to blow up once we armed the explosives. In the case of a derailed passenger train our only consolation was that the wreck blocked rail traffic on a strategic line and in this way reduced the dependability of the transportation system to serve German army needs.

WINDING UP

After a dash over a small hill where the random firing coming from the train could not reach us, Batko stopped and checked the readiness of everybody's weapons in case we would be ambushed on the way back at the next road crossing. He pulled out his revolver and said that he would now get rid of the Jewish kid who lost his detonator caps. I put my hand into my pants and pulled out a fistful of copper cylinders. With horror the

---

1   This event is also noted on p. 332 of the comprehensive *History of Partizans in Czechoslovakia, 1941-45*, published in Slovak by the PRAVDA Publishing Organization in Bratislava, 1984.

entire squad backed away. I completely forgot that even slight squeezing of the caps or landing hard on a stone would have exploded them. The caps were filled with picrate of mercury and each could blow a hole into my side. By some miracle, none of the caps exploded. The waterlogged soft field over which I hopped did not have stones. I guess there must have been a farmer nearby who must have been proud of his fine fields, which were kept up as if they were a garden.

Later I was told that Batko was only joking when he threatened to execute me, but I am still not sure about that, after witnessing incidents of how the Soviets enforced discipline.

That's how I became an expert in the derailing of trains and became finally accepted by the partizans as a fighter. I would be using such skills again as we made raids further up the Vah valley and later on the march going east.

Shortly afterwards, Batko and the squad were assigned to a new commander, a Ukrainian captain by the name of Bohinski, who happened to be a beast, although he was always smiling as he commanded men into suicide missions. We just kept moving in the northerly direction along the railroad to find places where the tracks were sufficiently close to the edge of a forest so that we could attempt another derailment and still manage to get away. As time passed the raids became more difficult because the Germans now placed a machine gun nest on a flat car ahead of the engine. Later, there was at least one case in which hostages were taken from villages next to our attack locations. That made it impossible to depend on the locals for food and for support. It increased the risks of mobile SS troops getting called in rapidly to hunt us as we marched away from the rail lines. But nothing in my entire partizan experience that ended in March 1945 ever approached the luck and the results of my first freight train at Opatova.

Partizan Ways

I came to admire the cool professional approach of Batko in all operational matters. Until we lost him, under incredibly stupid circumstances, we did not have enemy-caused casualties. Perhaps the main problem with the later attempts by the Slovak army to shift to partizan warfare was the absence of combat know-how to operate with improvised tactics. Regular army officers did not trust our motley band to stand up to Germans. I am convinced that if the uprising had been planned and then started as partizan warfare the military impact on the Allied war effort would have been greater and the casualties lower. Slovak staff officers who were in charge of the uprising were correct with regard to our irregular and uncoordinated methods. Nevertheless, the situation in the fall of 1944 made our ragtag squad vastly more effective than most army units.

Batko's training saved my life many times. For instance, he hammered unto us that at night immobile objects are hard to recognize, even when illuminated. In bad light, the enemy would first recognize only moving objects. Raking of the surrounding area with machine gun fire, a common practice by the Germans whenever we completed a nighttime raid, was primarily for the purpose of getting us sufficiently scared to start running and thus become more easily identified targets. His advice was to freeze at night or in dusk in a position, even if under fire, and to move only after the enemy believes that the partizans have disappeared. You had to have strong nerves not to run when under overwhelming fire.

Later I came to recognize the utility of following this rule, especially when I stood guard as a sentry. The trick for a sentry was to stand perfectly still not to be noticed and eliminated. This called for swiveling one's head back and forth so that one's eyes would continue to be stimulated as if in motion. Later, in winter, it was impossible for a sentry to remain immobile because the bone-crunching cold made anyone on guard duty stomp his feet and to hop around to keep warm. The Russians as well as the SS had specially trained snipers who could take out a sentry in darkness, illuminated only by starlight. During brilliantly clear moonlight nights, one could easily detect the silhouette of a sentry in motion from large distances. I always made sure to find a position where the bright moon projected a shadow against the snow.

LIBERATED CZECHOSLOVAKIA

Our rules were different from what was practiced in the now liberated territories that formed around the Banska Bystrica center of the uprising. Piled up into this retreat, surrounded on three sides by mountains, were most of the Jews who were still left in Slovakia, everyone who declared themselves as anti-Nazis, escaped prisoners including a large contingent of criminals released from prisons, and the Slovak army deserters. The liberated territory, following the Soviet political doctrine, was set up as a military enclave, which at the point of maximum expansion encompassed an area of about 8,000 square miles of mostly mountainous countryside. The army would then hold this enclave while the politicians would set up a Czechoslovak republic 300 miles from the front lines where the Soviet army had just halted.

The orders to the Czechoslovak army, now labeled as an Allied force, was to use conventional military tactics until the Soviet advance across the Carpathian mountain passes would materialize. The liberated area quickly acquired all of the pretenses of an organized state, including a legislature, a lively press, several radio stations, a military staff, train-based artillery, a liaison team from the U.S. Office of Strategic Services, and a judiciary. Delegations from London and Moscow were flown in and housed in hotels. B-17 bombers flew in from Italy in two sorties to unload arms and agents. The Russians transported in from Kiev two battalions of Slovaks who had defected to the Soviets in 1942 and had been trained in conventional warfare, Russian style.

Meanwhile, the Communist Party, claiming leadership because of the prospects of liberation by the Soviets, dominated a multiplicity of councils that became engaged in debates about military strategy with the representatives of the officer corps loyal to the London exile government. Looking back at the nine weeks of existence of the liberated territories I find the attempted pretenses of an organized government a laughable tragedy. Instead of preparing for the inevitable collapse the functionaries were pretending to gain importance by organizing for improving order.

When the temporarily liberated territories' defenses collapsed on the 28th of October under the onslaught of two German elite divisions withdrawn from the front in Poland, whoever depended on the fiction of surviving in the liberated territory was executed or deported to either prisoner-of-war camps (for regular Army soldiers) or to annihilation camps (for Jews). The troops that reoccupied mini-Czechoslovakia were especially merciless to Jews. Many of the still surviving Jews had emerged from hiding to take advantage of the freedoms of a liberated countryside.

Antitank ditches that were built to stop German panzers would become filled with bodies executed in mass killings after the collapse of the uprising. Had I remained with Kartal to leave for what he claimed to be a properly organized military operation instead of staying with Batko's small band I am sure that the chances of my ending in a mass grave would be very high. My instincts in this regard turned out to be right. Our loosely organized and quite undisciplined seven-man squad of miners clothed in motley civilian garments, wandering undetected from ambush to ambush, had more of a chance of surviving than the uniformed army.

The regular army spent more time trying to figure out the latest political rearrangements than in fighting. The army command apparently would not (or could not) admit that the uprising was doomed from its inception. When orders were finally issued in the last days of October to disperse into the mountains and to continue resistance by means of partizan warfare that came too late. The army had no pre-positioned bases in the mountains. They had no forward plans how to execute such a shift in tactics. Only the Soviet partizan command had the time and the organization to set up well-provisioned bunkers to where they could retreat on short notice when that became necessary.

My squad avoided most of the calamities that befell the Czechoslovak army. We were never hit by artillery or by bombs from airplanes. We avoided roads where German motorized infantry could overcome any resistance put up by the army. We learned how to carry our own supplies and how to live off the land. After a while there were no more informers among us who could betray our location. Lastly, our leaders knew where the pre-positioned hideouts were located so that we could always fade into the hills and survive, even in an extremely cold winter that made the regular Slovak army simply give up.

Experiences

Much of our time during the active combat period, from the time I joined the partizans until we were ordered to the winter quarters, was expended getting to and from a suitable spot where to place demolition charges. I am now a bit fuzzy about how often we have did that, but I think it was at least four times after Opatova. I remember vividly, however, some of the episodes on the way to and from our raids.

The Road Block

The partizan brigade command at that time was located in the ruins of what used to be a castle at Uhrovec. We received instructions that upon return from a train-derailing mission near Dubnica we should block a nearby road so that it would not be easily accessible by Germans in patrol cars. The standard approach for accomplishing that was to find a large tree on a curved road and knock it down with well-placed sticks of dynamite. The explosive charges would be set up so that the tree would fall across the roadway. Afterwards we would place one or two disk-like antitank mines among the branches to deter the removal of the tree. The trick was to hide the mines underneath the leaves and string thin wires from the needle-plunger detonator mechanism on the top of the mine to the spread-out branches of the fallen tree. When done, somebody had to crawl in among the branches and carefully remove the safety cotter pin from beneath the plunger. Batko had obviously done this many times.

A suitable oak tree was located and felled, and the mines were well placed. I helped in stringing the thin wires. After that I crawled carefully, very carefully, back to the roadway. As we were walking back to where we had previously set up a defense post against any surprises, a runner showed up on a motorcycle. He carried orders to remove the mines. There was another raiding party, from another command, coming down the already mined road and loaded with food and supplies.

After pausing for a long stream of Batko's colorful invectives, we trudged back to the oak tree, set up another defense position and slowly, but very slowly threaded the two safety pins back into the tiny holes separating the spring- loaded plungers from the detonation caps. We then departed, leaving the job of removing the huge tree from the roadway to the occupants of the truck presumed to be carrying the loot. As a practical joke, we made sure the returning party could never be completely sure that the pile of wood on the roadway was not still booby-trapped.

The brigade command did not thank us for that. We were reprimanded (with a smile) for "poor partizan discipline" even though we had performed a very dangerous job of laying the antitank mines and then removing them. Anyway, the entire incident enhanced our reputation as skillful operators.

The Banovce Ambush

After another raid on the railroad, we were hurrying back, as usual, to our base camp. There was always a possibility that the Germans or the Hlinka Guard would be dispatching trucks full of troops to intercept us as we crossed highways, usually without any cover. Our tactic was to walk as long as possible along the edge of a forest and then dash across the open land straddling a road until we could reach another cluster of trees on the opposite side.

The incident I describe here occurred in mid-October. As usual, we started relaxing a bit when we finally reached what we believed to be partizan-occupied territory near our base. We were walking along a cowpath behind a screen of hedges that blocked visibility from a highway that was beneath us in a valley. Suddenly there was an eruption of rifle and machine pistol fire on the highway below. It was accompanied by shouting and cries of men who must have been hit. A Slovak army officer with Czechoslovak insignia appeared, ordering us to move from our hidden position and deploy to the highway in order to block the escape of a fleeing Hlinka Guard detachment.

Apparently there were two truckloads of the hated Black Shirt Hlinka Guard troops headed for Prievidza in the direction of our brigade HQ. A mixed partizan and Slovak army group that had set up an ambush across the valley had just intercepted the Guards. The Guards had jumped out of the truck and set up defense positions in the roadway ditches while taking casualties.

From where we were located we could look directly down on the Guards hugging the roadside. They were firing on their attackers who were shooting from the top of the other side of the valley. Tato set up our light machine gun and emptied all of his magazines into the Guards who were now drawing fire both from the front and their back. I squeezed off the five rounds from the clip in my bolt-action rifle in the general direction of black uniforms although, in the total confusion, I had no way of knowing if I hit any. The Guards then started fleeing or were giving up, although I saw a number of men in black uniform motionless. Tato then took all of my surplus ammunition to reload his magazine to give the Guards a parting fusillade. By the time he had fully reloaded there were no more targets to be had. The fact that both Tato and I ran out of ammunition reflected the Soviet approach to special operations. Our carrying capacity was committed to explosives and survival gear in support of long, rapid marches and certainly not for engaging in firefights.

At this point, our group emerged from our cover in pursuit of the Guards who vanished around a road turn. Such action was something that we were prohibited from doing as a squad strictly dedicated to mining. As I ran, I lost one of my ill-fitting shoes but did not notice it at the time. Although bullets kept whizzing all around, I moved as fast as I could until a Russian I knew stopped me on the roadway. He ordered me to help carry one of the most popular Russian officers, one of the original parachutists, who was now lying in the roadside ditch, moaning in a puddle of blood. We made an improvised stretcher out of my green military coat and tried to lift the wounded man. I was horrified. His entire back was one huge gaping hole, with blood and pieces of lungs gurgling out profusely. All I could do was to take a piece of his shirt and press it into the hole. We had to move quickly because German armored cars could be arriving any moment to relieve the badly mauled Guards.

We carried the wounded man up the hill and then put him down. He was dead. Next day, during the funeral with full military honors I was recognized for assistance, although the entire episode was embellished by the story that the kid with only one shoe escaped injury in a hail of bullets by having his one shoe shot off.

Our squad was reprimanded again by the brigade commissar for getting involved in what he labeled as a poorly executed ambush. We had expended so much ammunition shooting at the Hlinka Guards that we were left without adequate firing power to protect ourselves in case we were attacked later. Batko was told that this was yet another example of his lack of "partizan discipline."

A Bungled Ambush

Following several incidents and near misses while moving to and from our raids, Batko decided that we would hide during daylight and walk only during nights. That could be done with only relative ease during full moonlight. On cloudy nights or when it rained, our progress would be very slow.

Late in October we were returning from what I believe was our last raid on the Trenčín-Žilina rail line. It was a miserable night. A cold and steady freezing rain soaked us to our skins. My new military coat, made out of heavy felt, was now heavy and smelly. The partizan-occupied territory had already shrunk to a few villages in the mountains. The former luxury of getting ferried by truck to and from our jumping-off points for raids was gone. The highways were now completely owned by German and Hlinka Guard patrol cars.

After slogging though brush Batko decided that we should keep moving along the road because we would never make it back to our base before daylight. It must have been after midnight when we heard the grinding of the gears of a truck coming up the hill ahead of us. Batko decided that capturing a truck would solve our transportation situation. As trained, we took up ambush positions behind trees, flipped off the safety switch on our weapons and got ready to toss hand grenades on the back of the truck while it was Tato's job to kill the driver and anyone on the driver's seat.

As the truck, with dimmed headlights, approached slowly our lead man tossed a Slovak concussion hand grenade on the top. It did not explode. Back from the truck came loud cursing in Russian. The occupants riding the truck were partizans being ferried to another location. Nobody was hurt except that Batko was called before the Division commissar for yet another reprimand.

Back in camp others poked fun at our trigger-happy band that had already earned a reputation for practicing unconventional warfare with high explosives. We were teased for our incompetence in getting even a hand grenade to work properly.

UPRISING DEFEATED

On the 28th of October, the SS troops that had been withdrawn from Poland wiped out the militarily untenable position of the Slovak defenses around Banska Bystrica, the command as well as the political center of the uprising. After finishing that engagement the Germans, their loyalist Slovak Army collaborators and the Hlinka Guards had ample military resources to pursue the Soviet-led partizans that had so far operated with only little interference from mountain bases or from relatively inaccessible settlements. The troops attacking us were mostly former prisoners of war, so-called Vlasov soldiers, named after the Ukrainian general who commanded anti-Soviet fighters. These men had expected that after the Germans' victory they would end up in positions of power in the Ukraine, Byelorussia, Lithuania and Estonia.

Vlasov's men had joined the Germans in 1941 and 1942 when putting on an SS uniform looked like an excellent choice and was certainly preferable to ending up in one of the German labor camps. German SS officers commanded these troops, above the battalion level. The SS viewed them as useful forces to do their dirty work, such as burning villages, executing hostages, and hunting Jews. Their official designation was "police action groups." In occupied lands, they applied extreme violence against civilians by means of torture, wanton murder and mass executions. Their specialty was the suppression of "bandits," which meant hunting us even in remote places where regular German troops would never care to go.

The SS police action groups were a collection of brutal and desperate individuals who had bargained their way out of the prison camps by turning into deadly anti-Jewish and anti-partizan detachments. As the end of the war approached, many of these non-German SS members were seeking refuge among the partizan units by claiming to be runaways from prisoner-of-war camps. Since most of the Slovak partizan groups were shattered after the collapse of the uprising, it was often impossible to distinguish whether a small group of men approaching you in the forest might be an SS reconnaissance team, remnants from a broken-up partizan brigade, or a few ex-Vlasov operatives pretending to be anti-Nazi fighters.

Throughout this period, I became keenly aware that misidentification of who was a partizan and who was not could make the difference between life and death. Most of the partizans had destroyed all of their identification papers that could have marked them for summary execution if caught by the wrong group. I retained my partizan identification papers throughout the entire ordeal. The papers were officially stamped on September 29th 1944 as issued by the Czechoslovak Army Command. As added insurance, I always carried a hand grenade in my clothing even while sleeping.

3. Partizan Identity Card

Losing Batko

I certainly owe my life to the wisdom and survival know-how of Batko, who somehow managed to get a motley collection of individuals to work as a band that could function effectively. Although I cannot tell for sure where I got this story, I heard that Batko was allowed to parachute drop into Slovakia as an alternative to a death sentence. That was a frequent case with many Soviet partizans who had originally avoided capture by the advancing German armies in 1941. Instead of getting killed by the Germans or their own commissars (who shot retreating soldiers), a few of these survivalists retreated into the woods and marshes of Byelorussia from where they waged effective partizan warfare for almost three years.

When the Russian front advanced into Poland, these partizans were brought before the NKVD (the Soviet political discipline enforcers). Anyone that was suspected of harboring independent views, or suspected as an anti-Soviet fighter, was either executed or sentenced to hard labor in Siberia. It appears that Batko became a too popular guerilla leader. He lost his left hand in combat although I suspect it must have been blown off by an accidental explosion from a fuse. That earned him another lease on life even though he was never fully accepted as one of the officers who were welcome at the Soviet brigade HQ. Batko was also known for his reckless courage, which earned him the job of heading the mining squad, certainly one of the most risky assignments you could be given in partizan warfare.

As early November set in, the members of our team, which never exceeded twelve men, were getting physically exhausted and quite sick. The skin on our feet became infected, which made walking increasingly painful. I could not hold down our food rations of bread and fried bacon. We had not washed for a while and while sleeping in haystacks we all picked up lice and fleas. For a while I did not have a good coat, since half of it was burned one night while I fell asleep too close to the embers of a campfire.

Then we lost Tato and Milos. Both were wounded and were left in one of the villages as we passed by, never to be heard of again, even after the war when I tried to locate them. A few Slovak members of our squad disappeared, without explanation, although we suspected that they saw the end coming and were looking for places to hide. In their stead, we gained one gypsy, one Ukrainian who claimed to have escaped from a prison train, and three Jews, including old Mr. Kolin, a WWI veteran and now close to sixty years old. Most of the men did not wish to let Kolin join us except for his pleasantly ingratiating personality and his treasure trove of sage advice that made everybody listen attentively. He just tagged along as we marched, did not carry a gun and refused to leave us. Ultimately, he took good care of increasingly touchy negotiations with villagers about food supplies and had imaginative ways of solving everyday small household problems. He became sort of a fussy grandmother to all of us. Batko, a soft soul behind all of the gruff cursing, did not have the heart to send him away to certain death.

Amazingly, old Kolin survived the tribulations of partizan existence after the fall of the uprising. I have no idea how he could possibly have done that. After the war, he came to visit me. It turned out that he was a remote relative of my sister's future husband.

One day, we were sent on a foraging mission. The purpose was to accumulate additional supplies to be stored in one of our hideaway shelters as the winter was approaching. Our practice of always staying off the roads and to keep walking at the edge of the woods did not do us much good. The leaves had already fallen and the countryside was bleak, with increasing difficulties for us to hide during our marches.

It was not far from Zavada when we saw a truck approaching towards us at a high speed. The squad took whatever cover we could, except that Batko, with his usual swagger, kept walking calmly in the center of the road, hefting his PPS machine pistol over his bad left arm. The machine gun placed on top of the truck cabin started firing at Batko, who kept running, firing continuously, to get closer to the truck so that he could hit the driver. Batko was cut down instantly. We managed to fire a few rounds at the truck as it reversed direction and disappeared behind a curve. To this day I do not know whether Batko's actions were calculated to destroy the truck or to give us sufficient time to get away.

Uprising Statistics

The key events in the abortive Slovak National Uprising, now glorified as a heroic liberation movement, can be summarized as follows:

August 28, 1944: Uprising begins

September 1, 1944: Germans disarm Eastern Slovak Army Command. The original battle plan is doomed.

September 6, 1944: The liberated Czechoslovak area declares its formation and announces the formation of a new government to rule the occupied territory.

October 28, 1944: Organized uprising liquidated, most of the Slovak forces disband and return to villages to hide.

October 28, 1944 – April 5, 1945: Fight continued by partizans in small groups. Russians, Jews, Communists and those Slovaks identified as leaders of the uprising remain in hideouts during the winter under conditions of extreme duress.

The rapid demise of the uprising should not be seen as only a marginal disturbance. Here are some statistics:

Slovak army + Volunteers at start = 60,000

Partizan battalions when uprising falters = 18,000

German SS uprising suppression troops = 40,000

Hlinka Guards loyal to Nazis = 20,000

Stories

The Soviet commanders applied brutal discipline to enforce security and political objectives as well as control though intimidation. At Soviet headquarters, there was always a sniper who was conspicuous for carrying a silencer attached to a semiautomatic Tokarev rifle, even while on duty at the headquarters, whereas partizan leaders carried PPS submachine guns. It turned out this officer was an enforcer and executioner. I witnessed one summary court martial of an escaped prisoner from a German camp who was accused of trying to infiltrate our ranks. He was led away by two men and followed by our ever-present officer with a silencer mounted on the muzzle. A short while later only three men returned.

My first encounter with the severity of the Soviet rules took place late at night at a campfire. In the prior afternoon we stopped a moving van that transported somebody's furniture. We searched the van for suitable items of clothing, such as underwear and any waterproof outerwear. In one of the drawers somebody found an old and loaded pre-WWI vintage revolver that was rusted. Since all of the members of our squad already had side arms, I was presented with the revolver, which would be of little use except to shoot myself with in case I got wounded. At the campfire, I started cleaning the weapon when it went off for reasons I am still not sure about. Luckily, the bullet whizzed over everybody's heads. The commissar came over and announced that this was my lucky day. If anyone had been wounded I would be executed on the spot. The revolver was confiscated and smashed with rocks.

The Nováky Incident

One of the saddest episodes from the history of the uprising concerns the dissolution of the Jewish Nováky battalion in the third week of September 1944. A force of young Jewish men marched into combat from their slave labor camp. They were immediately placed, without adequate weapons or training, to hold fixed positions against attacks by a highly experienced unit of the German mechanized infantry. After the Germans decimated and routed this unit, the remnants were placed under the Soviet partizan command, which was recruiting trusted civilians to enlarge the size of its forces.

As the remnants of the Nováky unit retreated into the hills they passed through a village. The soldiers, as was usually the case, stopped for a rest and looked for places where they could get some food from the locals. One of the men leaned his rifle against the doorpost as he entered into one of the peasant cottages. As I was told later, the partizan commander, Capt. Bohinski, happened to pass by. He saw the rifle leaning against the door. The entire Nováky group was then summoned and informed that a partizan may never part with a weapon. Although this rule was generally talked about, this was never taken too seriously and was never considered as an infraction punishable by death. The offending soldier was then promptly executed.

This episode, in different versions as to the details of who did what, was widely circulated and discussed in our dugouts. Since Bohinski was also our battalion commander and had inspected our group on two occasions, we were aware that even the fearless Batko was afraid of him. Capt. Bohinski always came always dressed in a mint-condition leather jacket and leather pants, with medals all over his overcoat, which our fighters considered to be ostentatious.

Later, in January, during retreat from a raiding party, we were hit with mortar rounds and Bohinski was wounded. Though we never carried our wounded, in the case of Bohinski we were ordered to make a stretcher and to carry him through hip-deep snow up a steep mountain face. The campfire scuttlebutt was that Bohinski was a high-ranking NKVD officer who was accustomed to using often capricious executions to reinforce Soviet control through terror.

The Lužna Incident

Terror was also applied to the villagers, although nowadays many of the occupants of hillside shelters receive generous pensions for services rendered in the uprising and are unwilling to talk about it. In February I found temporary shelter in the village of Liptovska Lužna. I had been sent there to look up an innkeeper who had the reputation of helping out partizans who needed warm quarters while recovering from illness. About two weeks later, the innkeeper's sister-in-law came running to the shed where I was sleeping, asking for my help because a band of four partizans were demanding money. When I confronted the band it was obvious that I had made a terrible mistake.

This was one of the many irregular gangs who were rampaging through the countryside towards the end of the war. Some of these were escaped criminals seeking legitimacy as freedom fighters. Others were turncoat Nazi mercenaries who tried to save their hides by tagging on to one of the many partizan groups roaming the hills. On the way, they were raping and killing. They lived off the land by means of intimidation of the terrified peasantry.

In front of a few assembled villagers, the leader of the gang informed everybody that I would be shot for interfering with the collection of essential supplies for freedom fighters. My hands were tied behind my back and I was led down the steps to the river, the usual execution grounds, with the villagers watching in silence. It looked to me that this would surely be my end.

At this moment coming up the road was a tall man I only knew as Lieutenant Rudo. Rudo was an ethnic German communist who had seen me a few times as a HQ sentry. The unique feature of Rudo was his machine pistol. Towards the end of the war some of the elite SS units were supplied with advance model rapid-fire large-caliber machine pistols made in Austria by Heckler and Koch. These were weapons that looked and functioned very much like the AK-47 weapon adopted by the Soviets fifteen years later. Rudo barked, "Let the kid go, he is one of ours" and identified himself as a senior partizan officer. The raiders then retreated to the inn, collected whatever cash and bottles of plum brandy they could find, and disappeared. Rudo reprimanded me for getting mixed up in local matters and ordered me to leave the village to return to the partizans. After the war, I looked up Rudo. He was now a full colonel in the new Czechoslovak army and the chief examiner of claims for restitution of prewar military rank by those who were suspected of collaboration with the Nazis.

Discussing "partizan discipline" in terms that always relate somehow to executions sheds a light on the harsh reality that many of the victims of the Slovak uprising were not necessarily from Nazi bullets. After the fall of the uprising many of the survivors, often aged Jews, women and children, sought refuge in remnants of woodcutters' huts or in caves for storing potatoes. I know of two families from Trenčín who found temporary shelter in such spaces only to be robbed and then murdered by bands that were also seeking a place where they could hide.

THE PIG AND THE PEASANT

One of my favorite stories from that period is that the Russians loved to send me into villages to seek out sources of food. Sometimes these villages were German-held and they were always filled with informers who called in the ubiquitous Ukrainian SS police who came in on motorcycles.

On one of these missions, I was dispatched late at night to check out a cottage that was at the corner of a settlement. As an armed partizan I was in a position to ask for a voluntary gift of food and if that was not granted to insist on it. Since this was already late in December, I am sure our starving comrades must have raided this settlement before. The peasant in the cottage I entered knew that he would have to give us something but pleaded, with increased agitation, that he had hardly anything left to feed his family for what remained of the winter. With all of the shouting going on in this one-room hut, we must have woken a pig hidden behind the stove. When I heard the pig snorting I became sufficiently annoyed to demand that we must get the peasant's pig. I knew that this animal would be the principal source of meat for the family for the rest of the winter. Peasants usually killed a pig around Christmastime and used up just about every part of it as a way of adding fat and bits of smoked meat to supplement their protein-poor diet, which was based mostly on potatoes, cheese and bread.

The peasant and his wife started crying, pleading for the life of the pig. They claimed that informers would surely find out that the partizans took the meat, since everybody in this tiny and pitifully poor settlement would know on the following morning that a pig was missing. The peasant pleaded that his family would be killed for feeding the partizans and their house burned down.

By this time, my other associates have arrived. I was then commanded to take out my Walther 9mm automatic pistol and shoot the pig in the head while the rest of the squad was restraining the increasingly distraught peasant and his screaming wife. We cut up the pig into quarters, left a few choice pieces and half of the meat for the family and started dragging our share of half of the pig back to the forest. The peasant must have been sufficiently experienced in such matters to ask for a receipt for the confiscated meat. So I wrote something like "Pavel Strassmann of the Czechoslovak Partizans hereby certifies that so-and-so gave us a supply of pork in support of the national liberation movement." To complete the documentation in an orderly manner, I asked how much the pig was worth? The peasant said, "It's worth everything I got." So I put down "50,000 crowns, signed Pavel Strassmann." That was a ridiculously large amount of money but that did not matter to me as long as we could get out of the settlement without a further incident.

In August 1945, I walked down through the street of Trenčín. I still carried an automatic pistol in my hip pocket, because the times were still uncertain and wartime scores were still getting settled. Suddenly I see this big, hulking peasant run across the square waving a big stick in my direction. I just put my hand on my pistol and flipped the safety lever, just in case. The guy embraced and kissed me. Apparently he took my receipt as well as other cleverly accumulated papers and was given by the government custody of a farm that had belonged to a Nazi collaborator. The fact that the farm was formerly expropriated Jewish property that was now distributed to the newly minted party faithful, as the spoils of war did not seem to bother anyone.

THE NOVÁKY JEWISH BATTALION

A definitive historical treatise should be written someday about the participation of Jews in the Slovak uprising. I have found too many unanswered questions about the organization and the fate of the armed unit that was formed on September 1 under Jewish command. These men and a few women organized a Jewish battalion under organized Czechoslovak army command.

Legally the Nováky Jewish unit was a uniformed Allied force, not an irregular collection of armed civilians, as was the case with the Jewish groups that had been operating principally in the forests of Lithuania and Byelorussia. This is an important distinction. So far as I can tell, the Nováky force was the first exclusively Jewish uniformed military unit engaged in combat since the destruction of a Jewish state by the Romans in 70 A.D. In fact, the Nováky unit preceded by a few weeks the formation of a much better known Jewish unit that became part of the British forces in Libya under the command of General Montgomery.

On the day of the uprising the arms that had been secretly stowed at the Nováky camp in walls and under the kitchen floor were broken out and distributed to selected squads of young men. The Hlinka Guard camp guards were disarmed as they fled. The local gendarmes unit also opened their armory to the Jewish inmates and provided additional weapons. About 200 then volunteered to join a newly formed combat unit.

The newly formed Nováky unit immediately proceeded to the nearest army base (at Prievidza) where everyone received Slovak army uniforms, Czechoslovak shoulder patches, light arms and a brief training session which involved one visit for rifle practice at a local firing range. The new unit included three former reserve officers from the prewar Czechoslovak army who assumed command on account of their military seniority.

A day later, the Nováky unit received orders from the now Czechoslovak Army HQ in Banska Bystrica to proceed to two nearby mining towns with a population consisting mostly of ethnic Germans. The Germans fled without a shot getting fired. The Army command now assigned the Nováky unit to take up fixed positions to prevent an oncoming Wehrmacht unit from occupying a critical rail junction. The ill-prepared and untrained defenders dug into shallow positions with the intent to follow conventional Slovak army defense tactics. They had rifles, light machine guns, a few heavy machine guns, a cannon, but no communication equipment except for runners. There were no rear echelon support units, no reserves and no artillery to support the Nováky unit's forward positions now emplaced in an open, flat valley.

The vastly more experienced Germans used tanks, armored vehicles, artillery, mortars and an observation aircraft to attack the Jewish lines of defense. As was the case with German combat units, their command and control relied on good radio connectivity to concentrate their attack. In the two attacks, involving artillery and mortar barrage, the Nováky Jewish unit lost over 20 percent of the unit killed and a much larger number wounded before disintegrating as an organized unit. I found out about this battle only a day later when I heard that a number of wounded from Trenčín was housed in a local inn. There I found my cousin (twice removed) Erich Politzer, a talented pianist, in a sorry state. He was bandaged up and bleeding profusely, with no prospects of recovery. Three days later we had to abandon that village, thus leaving the wounded to their fate.

THE SURVIVING JEWS

When the Jewish fighters went to war, the rest of the camp population, mostly women, children and those without any combat capabilities, were encouraged to flee back to the communities from where they had been originally deported. Such guidance was offered on the assumption, subsequently proven terribly wrong, that the Soviet army would be coming soon to the rescue of the uprising, which would bring liberation and freedom. Unfortunately, wherever the Jews leaving the labor camps departed for locations that were subsequently involved in combat between the partizans and the SS units, only tragedy waited for them. This misfortune was further compounded by the migration of Jews into the territories that had been taken over by the uprising. Many of these Jews had so far remained hidden from persecution or lived in relative safety under the cover of false identity papers. When captured after the uprising collapsed, they were executed. Those who remained in the Nováky or the Sered camps were deported to annihilation camps where the probability of survival was marginally better than the fate of those who were misled to believe that the uprising brought their salvation.

A Military Judgment

In retrospect I place much of the blame for the unnecessary casualties in the uprising on the leadership that placed men, whether trained or not, to take fixed front-line positions against overwhelming German forces that were well organized and well equipped for such actions. Identical mistakes were repeated during the initial enthusiastic phases of the uprising. Very soon, however, it became apparent that the Soviet relief forces would never show up. Whatever battle positions were taken up by the regular Slovak army, the defenses quickly melted away as soon as the Germans attacked. The Slovak army did not have the stomach for heroic stands.

Partizan casualties were also high in conducting ambushes on Germans and on the Hlinka Guard in the absence of any wireless communications except for links from the Soviet partizan battalion HQs to the central partizan command in Kiev.

Our losses kept mounting with the onset of the winter not only from bullets but also from disease and freezing. Nevertheless, the chances of surviving in a mobile partizan unit were always better than those of an unsupported foot soldier under artillery fire and facing tanks.

The fundamental doctrine of all partizan warfare is to avoid becoming a target. The units, which fought using conventional military tactics, could not succeed. They gave the Wehrmacht a target-rich shooting gallery from where they could proceed to kill the Slovaks methodically and from a safe distance.

An Assessment

At this point, it is important to comment on the significance of the distinctions between the former Slovak Nazi-supporting army (since 1938), which partially transformed itself into an Allied Czechoslovak army as result of the uprising in August 1944, whose remnants became Czechoslovak partizan units after October 1944.

From the standpoint of the rules of war the Slovak military, after 1938, were traitors and committed supporters of the Nazis. They were the sole participants in the Germans' attack on Poland. They were engaged in major combat against the Soviet Union. The Slovak state had formally declared war on the Allies, including Britain and the USA. Consequently, all officers of the Slovak army could be considered enemies who could be dealt with under then prevailing rules of war, which the Soviets applied ferociously and cruelly. As I see it, the entire Slovak uprising, premature or not, had as its primary purpose the recasting of an army recognized as traitors of Allies to an army that would benefit from the gains of the Allied victors as soon as the war ended. Accordingly, it was hoped that the Slovak army would not suffer any of the penalties of the losers if the Slovak uprising became recognized as an Allied military action.

When judged from a historical perspective, the failed Slovak uprising was a success, especially as seen from the standpoint of the officers of the Slovak army. Only a very small number of the most vocal supporters of the Nazi regime in the Slovak army were ever dismissed. If punished at all, that was only through early retirement, with pensions.

Mountains

Before the fall of the center of the uprising in Banska Bystrica our own skirmishes took place only on a limited scale. Encounters were precipitated either by raiding parties of local Hlinka Guards or when we ran into an exchange of fire on the way to or from a raid. Casualties were very light. Most of the firing was from light arms or occasional bursts from a submachine gun. Twice we were subjected to a few rounds of 3.5-inch mortars that missed us.

Until October 20 the weather in Western Slovakia was tolerable. Afterward it started snowing at the higher elevations where we remained most of the time. Our footprints in the snow now left traces about our movements. Compounding this vulnerability was the loss of the leaf cover from the largely deciduous forests. This limited our ability to make fires because smoke could be readily seen from miles away by an occasional Fiesler-Storch observation plane that could radio our position to the Germans. Finding a coniferous growth of trees was now necessary. Fir trees offered a better cover. They were also a source of branches that could be laid on top of the snow to insulate us from freezing solid to the ground whenever our body heat melted snow as we tried to snatch some sleep.

The needles and the pitch-filled twigs found in coniferous forests were also useful as quick fire starters when we needed to warm up in the chilling wind and all other wood was wet and frozen. To this day walking in a pine forest covered by pine needles gives me more pleasure than viewing even the most fancy rose garden. Where I live now I have three small stands of tall pines with the ground covered by a thick layer of yellow pine needle mulch. While I was absent during one of many trips my overly fastidious groundskeeper decided to replace the pine mulch with the more decorative shredded tree bark. When I returned, I had the expensive tree bark raked out and the pine needles replaced.

The Base

Immediately after the fall of Banska Bystrica our situation changed radically. Previously we could walk through forests with hardly any interference. Experienced commando raiders who came well equipped with radios and who had the benefit of local intelligence from informers now hunted us. I suppose that the Germans also relied on information that was extricated by torture from captured partizans.

Until the end of October, we remained reasonably safe if we occasionally treated ourselves to the luxury of camping for the night in a remote and well-guarded place. We preferred to stay in villages located at the end of narrow valleys, especially if such a village was accessible only through a long and narrow winding road. Our command assumed that positioning sacrificial sentries at the points where an approaching vehicle could be detected would give us sufficient time to escape into the woods. Our favorite villages for overnight stays were Trebichava, Zavada and Čierna Lehota.

Meanwhile, following time-tested partizan experience, our commanders had made arrangements to set up what were believed to be defensible dugouts on the top of two mountains, Čierny Vrch and Rokoš, where we would retreat when attacked.

During the raids on the railroads, we kept moving from improvised camping grounds, with occasional stays in abandoned cottages, barns or haystacks, when we were lucky to find them. In 1944 peasants stopped collecting the hay, which was mowed and then stored during the summer, from the meadows in the mountains. After the fighting broke out the peasants and the shepherds would not venture to visit upland pasturelands. As a sufficiently large pile of accumulated hay rotted it generated heat from fermentation. The warmth was particularly helpful in the winter. The only disadvantage of sleeping in such a haystack was picking up fleas and lice during an overnight stay as the few remaining haystacks became frequented by passing partizans and refugees from occupied districts. Despite that experience, to this day I still have a liking for the smell of rotting grass.

Severe winter weather, followed by blistering snowstorms, arrived on the mountains after the first week in November. At the time, we did not know it but it would deliver the coldest weather in more than ten years in a country where winters are usually cold and long. When I asked to visit my former battlegrounds with an escort from the Slovak military in mid-May of 1993 I inquired about suitable clothing to wear on excursions from the car. I was told to bring knee-high boots and a padded jacket because it was still snowing on the mountain range that had been the location of one of my encampments.

Retreat to the Mountain

The planned retreat to the prepared base on the Čierny Vrch took place sometime in the second week of November. As was our custom, we tried to stay overnight in one of the outlying villages because food and water were more accessible in such places. We posted two sentries on the road leading to the village, which was Zavada. The forward sentry would fire at any approaching vehicle and the backup sentry would then alarm us to get out.

We miscalculated. The attack force was obviously well trained in dealing with partizans. Instead of coming up the road, they walked around the village and set up mortar positions to fire at the escaping partizans after the sentries set off the alarm. We were now without Batko but had enough sense to get our squad lodged at the farthermost end of Zavada. When the shooting began we started running up the hill towards the Čierny Vrch. Although we had to pass through an open pasture to disappear into the nearest woods the shrapnel from the Nazi mortars missed everyone. You hugged the ground when a mortar shell was launched and got up to run after the round landed. I believe that the mortar fire was launched primarily to pin down those partizans who could not run or those who just kept running propelled by fear instead of good tactics. After the war, I visited Zavada and saw a memorial to those who were killed on that fatal day. The casualties were mostly villagers, not partizans. The purpose of the Germans was to terrorize through murder and mass reprisals the villagers who had supported the partizans.

When we finally reached the dugouts on top of the mountain, we were amazed by their clever construction. It would take direct bomb hits or artillery to destroy them. The approach paths were narrow and easily defended if you had a sufficient number of men ready to make a last stand to stop the approaching raiders.

The base had three dugouts, smelly but warm and reasonably dry. Our original Batko squad was broken up. I was assigned to the foraging group, whose objective was to accumulate as much food as possible before descent into the valley, through deep snow, would become too difficult.

The base was well organized. Stragglers as well as men of questionable background were not accepted. In one case, a man suspected of being a spy was shot. Particularly tragic was the rejection of several Jewish families who were seeking protection from the partizans. They were either former inmates of labor camps in Slovakia or, in one instance, a family that left a hideout to welcome the newly liberated Czechoslovak territory. So far as I know all of these families perished.

Rations were handed out twice daily. They consisted mostly of bread, smoked bacon, sugar, slivovitz and cigarettes. The cook for each dugout also received the meat and the cooking ingredients to prepare a meal. The food consisted mostly of boiled pork with cabbage and potatoes, all of which was generously doused with paprika.

It is on the Čierny Vrch where I acquired the habit of claiming my full rations as a partizan, which included cigarettes and slivovitz. I traded the cigarettes for bread, which convinced me never to smoke after I noticed how starving men were willing to forgo life-sustaining food for their addiction. Initially, I accepted my rations of liquor and started drinking it on long treks from the mountains. After I found that alcohol made me dizzy I gave it up and exchanged it for extra bacon, which provided more calories per pound of carrying weight than any other source of food.

THE AMERICAN

One evening, a Czechoslovak officer came into the dugout and asked for anyone who spoke English. In view of my smattering of English I volunteered and was immediately assigned to guard a dark-skinned man in civilian clothing, who claimed that he was a U.S. airman who had been shot down. The American gunner was on his way to Banska Bystrica to be picked up for a return to his base in Italy. This was an incredible story for us, although after the war it proved to be correct. Indeed, American B-17s landed in Banska Bystrica twice to deliver American intelligence emissaries and American weapons and to return with fifty-six American airmen to their safety near Bari in Italy. The only problem was that our airman would not make it back until after liberation because the US Army Air Force by that time stopped flying to Slovakia after the sole liberated airfield was occupied by the Germans.

Why the airman had to be guarded all night was beyond my comprehension until I found out later that there was always a conflict about the handling of Americans between the army officers, with allegiance to the London-based Czechoslovak government in exile, and the Russian political command. The Soviets tried to deny to the Slovaks any contacts with the American military.

Since the Slovaks (now the "Czechoslovak Allied Forces") traded American fliers for political and military recognition, the local senior Slovak officer did not wish for any harm to come to my American. Perhaps the real reason was the rumor that all American fliers had gold coins sewed into their jackets to pay off locals after they were shot down. Forty-five years later, while serving in the Pentagon, I found out that this rumor was correct except that a small supply of gold coins was given mostly to officers. At any rate, the Russians had murdered an English reporter who had parachuted to write about partizan life. The reporter was killed after a Russian tried to take his jacket. As an excuse the reporter was accused of spying and carrying gold to set up a counterrevolutionary operation.

Years later, I related my airman story to Air Force generals during a Pentagon lunch. They found the missions of B-17s landing 350 kilometers behind German front lines, on grass covered airstrips to fetch American fliers under such circumstances, not plausible. I certainly had no verifiable proof about such adventures.

It so happened that sometime in 1990 I was invited to a fund-raising party for Senator John McCain, then contemplating to run for the presidency. Sitting next to me was a spry elderly gentleman. As conversation goes at such affairs, the topic of war service came up ("Where were you during the war?"). It turns out that this gentleman was a holder of the Flying Cross. He said that he flew one of the pilot pick-up missions to Banska Bystrica. This encounter resulted in my gaining access to the records of the 483rd Bomber Command and the identification of George Fernandes, of Portuguese origin, as the man who had been temporarily in my custody in 1944. I called George, now an invalid, at the VA hospital in Bellevue, Washington, and we had a pleasant chat. Poor George only remembered to having been well fed at a mountain top partizan base.

Subsequently, I delivered several lectures about the involvement of the American airmen and about the disastrous OSS mission (Office of Strategic Services, the predecessor of the CIA) in Slovakia in 1944. From what I have learned since then, the Cold War had already started in the middle of WWII. I could demonstrate that by describing how an American airman had to be guarded by an armed sentry to protect him from harm by the Russians.

GATHERING FOOD

We stayed on top of the Čierny Vrch for about a month. During that time, my squad was dispatched on weekly sorties to nearby villages to buy food or, if necessary, take it forcibly. To come down from the mountain over snow and then to learn whether a village was safe took most of a day. It took another day or more to collect the food and then another day to climb back up the steep and icy slopes.

Our preferred food sources were pigs, and when these were not available we settled for sheep. In one instance we also took a goat. The critters were skinned and then cut into quarters while we were still in the village. After that, each of us would carry one slab of meat up the hill back to the base. Getting orders to take one of such trips was a privilege. While we were in the village, we were able to stuff ourselves with food and then to wash. Still, while in the village, we were under continuous threat that the Germans or the Hlinka Guards would suddenly show up. After a while our visits started forming a pattern, which would set us up for getting intercepted.

I remember one such incident. I had just finished checking out a barn where we would be bringing a pig for slaughter. Instead of walking on the cow-path behind the houses I stepped right in front of a road intersection. There, gazing at me from a motorcycle sidecar, with a machine gun mounted on a swivel mount, sat a soldier in a grey-blue SS uniform. Had I started running, I am sure that he would have cut me down with a few bursts. Luckily, I carried my rifle upside down and behind my shoulder, which must have confused my appearance and was surely a sorry sight in my bedraggled overcoat. My hat was that of a local farmhand. While the German examined me, I slowly turned around and disappeared through the gate of a nearby garden, taking great care to close down the gate without showing any haste.

After that encounter, I abandoned the idea of picking up any meat that afternoon and made my way to the assembly point for the return up the mountain. The other partizans had received earlier warnings that the Germans were coming. The message never got to me.

CRIMES

It is impossible to talk about the partizan experience without mentioning the criminality that accompanied such activities. It is a fact that after the uprising all jails in the liberated districts were set open. As a result, there was a large influx of recruits to the armed resistance, which the criminals found rewarding to join. The aggressiveness and the stealth of the criminal element suited guerilla warfare very well. With small bands of desperadoes ranging through the countryside and law enforcement disappearing, there were unlimited opportunities to rob and pillage with impunity. If the victims could be marked as Nazi sympathizers, theft or murder could be called a patriotic act.

I became involved in a civilian murder as a bystander on one of the food-gathering trips to one of the villages. As we descended from the mountain and approached the village we saw a large moving van stuck in a ditch. The door of the van was open and a partizan band, then operating in the neighborhood, was rummaging through the contents that was filled with furniture and all sorts of household property. Standing next to the van was a man and a woman who were apparently the owners. The woman was getting very excited and was crying and shrieking in a loud voice that could be heard over quite a distance. Perhaps she said something threatening, but when she lurched at the leader of the partizans, he shot her in the head. When the husband jumped to catch the woman, he was also killed. After that we were invited to approach and help ourselves to some of the furs in the van.

One of the men from the partizan band that held up the moving van ended up becoming a member of the communist party leadership in Trenčín after the war, even though he had a prewar criminal record. Rumors started in 1947 that some of the partizans could be prosecuted for crimes committed during the war. I became apprehensive about possible consequences if I would have to appear as a witness. In a chance meeting on the Trenčín main square during Christmas holidays in 1947 this man casually mentioned to me that I would be well advised, as the son of a prominent capitalist, to get out of the country soon because when the communists take over, I would surely get into trouble. This risk was one of the many other reasons why I finally decided to get out of Slovakia before the communists takeover, which turned out to be in February 1948, ten days after I arrived in England.

Although I did not think so at the time, this ex-criminal's warning served me well. I should have seen it as a great favor rather than a threat.

BATTLE OF MAGURA

The few weeks of staying in the Čierny Vrch dugouts were stressful, hard, cold and demoralizing but relatively peaceful as compared with the fate of those who had escaped from Banska Bystrica after the uprising collapsed. There was a daily routine and nobody was starving. Medical care took care of most of the minor injuries, which were mostly skin scrapes that could easily transform into painful infections. The disastrous news about the collapse of the uprising trickled up to us slowly. Only the Soviet team and their radio operator knew what was really going on, but they were not sharing that with us. We considered ourselves lucky that we avoided the fate of those who were captured. According to our leaders, victory was just around the corner, although nobody could tell us when or where the Soviet army would be finally crossing the Carpathian Mountains to liberate us. As added relief, our dugouts became less crowded as many of the Slovaks did not return from sorties into the surrounding villages.

Meanwhile, our position was getting precarious as the villages from where we had obtained supplies were falling under the tightening control of well-organized patrols that were summoned by local collaborators as soon as any partizans showed up to collect food.

I believe it was in the second or third week of November that we were roused from sleep in the middle of the night and commanded to prepare ourselves for an immediate abandonment of our dugouts. An imminent attack was expected on our position. We packed whatever previously accumulated supplies we could carry and started on a march, in a single column, not knowing where we were going except that it would be in the direction of the advancing Soviet armies.

It is noteworthy to remark here about the partizan ways of marching. We always moved in a single file that was stretched out sufficiently so that an ambush or concentrated fire would kill as few as possible. Who would be walking "at the point," or in front of the file where most of the casualties would be suffered, was dictated by the most senior officer who was usually somewhere in the front. The marching order became more important as the depth of the snow increased. The first man in the rank would be hip-deep in snow and had to expend extraordinary efforts to stamp out a fresh passage. The tail end of the file was where the laggards and the sick would straggle. They were left to advance the best way they could, but rarely with any help.

In a long line we descended Čierny Vrch and crossed to ascend an even higher mountain, the Magura, where another partizan command HQ was located. We crossed the valley between the two mountain ranges and the road between in broad daylight, which made no sense, but I was in no position to ask questions. As we marched, other partizan groups were joining us. I had never seen hundreds of partizans marching as a group.

After reaching the top of the Magura early in the evening, we continued on a narrow path that ran along the ridgeline of the Mala Fatra mountains. It was still snowing. We had been already marching rapidly for twenty hours without a stop. I was somewhere near the middle of the line.

The Ambush

Suddenly shots came from automatic weapons in front of me and I could see muzzle flashes. That meant that we had run into an ambush, although I could not believe that our pursuers would do something like that at night, on top of a mountain. I saw figures moving about in what looked to me like white camouflage. That was a sure sign that German forces specializing in winter warfare had attacked us. Acting instinctively, I clutched my rifle and rolled down a steep slope to my right. As I spun downwards I must have lost much of what I carried in my backpack, including spare hand grenades, food and a half of my canvas tent. I slid down about a hundred feet when a tree finally stopped me. Crouching behind the tree I paused to observe what was happening.

Above me there was wild shooting and shouting. In a few minutes another partizan came rolling down the slope. It was Hatlancik, a partizan from Trenčín. He said that an ambush had been set up on the path on top of the ridge. We were now being pursued by what sounded like Ukrainian Vlasov SS troops speaking Russian and pretending to be our comrades. Hatlancik said we had to get away and not respond to the calls from the top of the ridge despite commands to climb back and rejoin the march. The calls were punctuated by spotty firing from small arms, which convinced me that returning to the top of the ridge was too risky.

Hatlancik and I then continued running down the steep slope of the mountain for a while until we came to the bottom of the ravine to a brook. On the opposite side there was another steep slope upwards. Now the shooting could be heard from all sides except from the direction ahead. We plunged into the ice-cold water and waded across. By now I was soaked up to my waist. How we climbed up to the top of the slope of the valley and how we continued marching away I do not remember. Hypothermia was now setting in, my teeth were chattering and I had a hard time walking or even thinking.

Months later, I found out that only a few partizans managed to escape the trap that had been laid by the Germans who organized this action as a way of destroying several partizan units in a sweeping encirclement. The German command used the proven tactic of dislodging partizans from multiple locations and then driving them into a "knapsack" where they could be surrounded and eliminated by superior firepower. With the exception of the deep ravine through which Hatlancik and I crawled out, all other sides of the mountain were cut off by German units operating from roads that blocked other escape routes.

Shattered Brigades

The surviving companions reassembled at the few remaining shelters that could be found in the bone-crunching cold. We could not depend anymore on finding quarters within villages now crawling with Hlinka Guard informers. All that was left were mountainside sheds for hay.

The Germans torched any structure they could find, but there were always sufficient sheds left for the partizans to seek out. How we managed to live under such unsanitary conditions without contracting typhus or another infectious disease while drinking water from polluted sources is a miracle. Since we operated in only small bands of fewer than a dozen fighters, the opportunities for an epidemic were limited. Anyone who got even modestly sick would not be able to keep up on our marches through snow. Even if infected with a communicable disease they could not transmit the contagion to too many.

Orders were now passed on to the survivors that remnants of the partizan brigades should reassemble for a march to the camps that were located eastwards on top of the mountain range in central Slovakia. This would necessitate descending from our higher elevations into the open and flat Turiec valley. After that we would have to climb up the steep slopes to get on top of the ridge line of the Lower Tatras which would take us marching about 100 kilometers closer to where the Soviet and the exile Czechoslovak armies were slowly pushing, with heavy casualties, their way through the Dukla pass leading from the Ukraine.

The marching ordeal started sometime in the second week of December. It required us to slog through hip-deep snow. We had to cross two open plains during nights to avoid an ambush from Germans who had already figured out the direction of our movements. The only question left was whether we would have to wade through water to cross the valleys, or if some unguarded bridges were still open for us to cross without getting soaked. Crossing the Turiec was accomplished over a bridge, even though we had to run to get away from the nearby highway and railroad tracks in case the enemy was alerted to our passage.

I cannot describe the effort and the strain involved in this march. We were wet and hungry and suffered from extreme cold and fatigue. My feverish condition returned, and I marched without much awareness about the surrounding except to follow the backpack in front of me. Although I was still lugging my rifle, I am not sure I would have had the strength to load, aim and fire it with any accuracy. As I recall it, only about half of the men who had started the march arrived at our final destination. Many just gave up and wandered to sides to sit down for a rest while the line of partizans passed by. Those who fell asleep from exhaustion froze to death. Quite a few just waited and then walked to the nearest village to give themselves up. Such choices were unacceptable to me.

Perhaps the most vivid recollections from this ten-day march were visions that kept me walking without collapsing. To prevent my mind from drifting into despair I developed what would become a recurrent dream-like fantasy visualizing the perfect life after the war. My brain kept generating movie-like images such as walking on streets of a great city with skyscrapers, riding in automobiles to visit gardens and standing in front of a beautiful house from where my mother was calling not to be late for Passover dinner. After a few days I could generate such scenes as it pleased me. I could even replay my favorite "virtual experiences." Once, when my babbling became too excited I was asked what the matter was. In my feverish abandon, I explained that I was on my way to America. Subsequently I would explain to everyone who would listen that the purpose of the entire march was to get me to America where I was already expected.

Years later, it was explained to me that such hallucinations were not unusual under conditions of extreme deprivation. In many cases it was such flights from reality that kept an individual strong enough to cope with adversity. It was a world of dreams that made people carry on without sinking into desperation that would otherwise make them give up under circumstances of otherwise unbearable reality.

Prašiva

After the ambush on the Čierny Vrch we were pushed to retreat to higher elevations while moving steadily eastward to get closer to where the central partizan command was located. There we could find shelter in underground structures that had been adopted from the Russian *zemlyanka* practice to seek survival under harsh winter conditions in as deep a hole in the ground. These cramped, hastily constructed, continually leaking ditches were always filled with the smoke-choking stench from cooking and fumes leaking from an improvised stove. Erected under improvised circumstances, these were partially collapsing structures at all times as the supporting earth-and-ice-covered-branches roofing kept falling in. The roofing timbers were lashed together with rope and were then covered with fir branches, which sometimes caught fire. These hideouts held two or three layers of sleeping platforms, packing as many troops as possible. There was hardly any space left for a passageway except for a small space at the entrance left for storing weapons. The latrines were located quite a distance away downhill.

Life in the Zemlyanki

Most of the zemlyankas that managed to last through the winter were constructed and maintained under the supervision of a *Sibiriak* (someone from Siberia) with experience in how to organize a defensible camp in deep snow. The entire camp would be placed among fir trees. The dugouts would also offer protection as bomb shelters.

After snowdrifts blocked access to roads that could have allowed German motorized troops to get closer to our mountain hideouts, a large number of the still surviving partizan forces were kept from freezing to death by huddling into these mountaintop camps. By the end of December, my unit finally settled down from marches proceeding from shelter to shelter to end on top of the Prašiva (dusty) Mountain. Here was a large complex consisting of more than six dugouts, each housing about thirty to forty starving, exhausted, and lice-infested remnants of the uprising.

After the war, I was told that the Prašiva zemlyanka compound had been constructed and well stocked with food weeks before the collapse of the uprising. They were to house the Soviet partizan supreme command after the inevitable SS attack would take place. I suppose that this explains why the Russian command zemlyanka, with a separate sentry, always emitted a delicious smell of cooking and why rowdy drinking parties could be heard sometimes late into the night while we were trying to fall asleep with our stomachs growling from discomfort.

Sleeping in the command quarters were few women who had tagged along with the top Soviet officers during the retreat from Banska Bystrica. These exceptionally well-groomed ladies were never seen carrying a weapon. They were rather distinct in that they were dressed in leather clothing that was always viewed as a sign of higher status. You could always tell a Soviet commissar by his leather jacket.

The Russian command post was off limits to us because it also housed a radio transmitter, which was our only contact with the outside world. Otherwise, there was little contact between the Slovaks and the Russians. I accepted that because I respected the Russians' combat, survival, and organization skills that were far superior to what we got from the leadership of the Slovak army. I suppose most of the Soviets were also survivors of Stalin's regime. These were very tough men. I admired their incredible stamina and their singing in chorus that started when we were ready to faint from fatigue during a march. To this day, I credit the experienced Russian leadership as the reason why I managed to survive at all.

I was lucky to be assigned to a zemlyanka for feeble partizans who somehow managed to make it up to the top of the mountain through waist-deep snow and under occasional enemy fire. Most of us were disabled from exhaustion and from frostbite. With the exception of a Russian captain, whose leg had to be amputated, I do not ever recall carrying with us any wounded. I doubt it if anyone who had been wounded would have ever made it through the ordeal of marching to the top of the Prašiva.

Our dugout housed three Jewish doctors. Two, Elo Luža and Imre Blau, were young and helpful. There was an older gynecologist from Bratislava whose name was, I believe, Wertheim, who took care of the camp followers. The Russians wanted to make sure that their kept women were not diseased. This arrangement had many advantages, including the fact that the Russians always gave the doctors extra rations, which they shared. Elo, always a practical joker, and who was suspected of being merely a medical student and not an MD, was in charge of rationing scarce medical supplies.

Most important was the access given to the doctors to an extremely hard-to-get supply of sulfa-drug antibiotic medication, which was extremely effective in arresting an infection from the frostbitten skin from spreading further as it kept festering. During my ninety-day easterly marches from the Inovec Mountain range near Trenčín to the Prašiva, my feet never managed to get completely dry. My shoes were full of holes and instead of possessing socks I wrapped each leg with strips of linen. These improvised socks kept slipping while I walked and created sores wherever the cloth edges rubbed against my skin, which became soft and peeled off easily. It did not take long before most of the skin below my knees was one large infected raw sore. Without the sulfa powder sparingly applied every day, I do not think I would have ever walked again as the infected skin became extremely sore. I had seen others with gangrene-like wounds before they fell to the wayside. I believe that there were more partizan casualties that resulted from freezing to death after taking a brief respite than from German bullets.

During the day, the repairs to the ever-collapsing dugouts fully consumed whatever energies we had. When it snowed, and that was frequent, we had to clear the space for holding frequent stand-up reviews by the commanders. Such time-consuming reviews, in gut-penetrating cold, were justified as a way of accounting for everyone as a security measure. We also had to clear the snow from where we kept stockpiling firewood.

4. The Prašiva Mountain Range in Winter

Since the top of the Prašiva was above the timber line and most of the existing trees nearby had already been cut down to construct the dugouts, the most difficult and time-consuming effort of the week involved marching down from the top of the mountain to reach one of the steep gulches where fir trees were still standing. The frozen trees were cut into luggable pieces with huge lumberjack-size two-man crosscut saws biting into hard-frozen tree trunks. That often felt like we were cutting metal, not wood. The individual pieces were then pulled up the hill with ropes lashed to our shoulders. The most convenient and surely the wettest way of accomplishing that was to do the dragging over the bed of an iced-over creek. Once a tree trunk was finally pulled up to the top it was then cut into small pieces and then chopped into oven-size pieces with axes. The green, frozen wood was poor fuel, since much of the fire was consumed in defrosting it and evaporating the water from the ice within. The wood burned because there was sufficient pitch in the pinewood to keep up the combustion. That was adequate to make the limited space in the dugout full of smoke but pleasantly warm. All of our heat, all cooking and all drinking water (from pots containing melted snow) came from a single cast-iron stove.

Living Conditions

The embers in the stove also served a unique sanitation purpose. Since everybody was full of lice, those of us who were more fastidious and could not tolerate the hundreds of little crawling beasties all over our bodies, had learned how to take the cleaning rods out of our rifles and to make their tips red-hot. Applying the tip of the steel rods to the seams of our clothing, where the lice and their eggs (the nits) gathered, roasted them without scorching our underwear too much.

Only the Russians in the command dugout had the rare facility for taking a steam bath to cleanse themselves. We did not. The best way in which we could limit the vermin was to exterminate the rapidly breeding population of lice down through nightly burning.

I did not get finally deloused until I was finally processed into the Czechoslovak Army in the town of Poprad on about April 1. At that time my entire body was completely shaved and depilated, showered and then doused with a profuse dusting with white powder that made me sick for days. That was a happy day.

Much of the time in the dugout was spent trying to get some sleep during the long nights in December and January. The only entertainment I recall during this time was the often-repeated dramatic performances by Elo Luža and an occasional singing performance by a young Russian accompanied by a harmonica. Though I was still suffering from fever, extreme fatigue and perpetual hunger, Elo's stories became memorable because they always centered on food and women. It appears that Elo, as a student, made a tourist trip to Paris prior to the war. There he must have acquired an especially vivid as well as perfect memory of each menu offered in the best restaurants, how the dishes were served and how the food was prepared. Although the entire dugout was in a state of modest starvation, Elo was asked on particularly trying nights to talk about one of his epicurean adventures. These always ended with a course of snails served with garlic. After such an imaginary dinner Elo embarked on an elaborate description of his adventures during a visit to a Parisian bordello. I did not understand most of the fine points of his explanations.

Although Elo was once threatened of getting shot for his ribald narratives nobody could ever get enough of his fantastic adventures. He was asked for encore performances frequently. As conditions deteriorated his most popular story featured a dinner he would be personally serving to the occupants of our dugout immediately after liberation. It was not the food but the details about the first day after the end of the war that appealed to everybody's imagination.

It is worth noting here that when May 5th, the day of liberation, finally arrived, I could not notice much of a difference in my surroundings except that there was a major change in the way I had to start thinking about the world. Until Victory, I could focus on the only thing that mattered, which was survival. After Victory, everything became possible, which was quite a burden to place on a sixteen-year-old.

Escaping Execution

The worst incident for me, while trying to survive as a partizan, took place late in January. By then I had fever most of the time and my feet were infected from wounds that even the sulfa drugs could not cure. After surviving on a diet of smoked pork fat and an occasional chunk of pickled uncooked liver, I could not hold food in my digestive system. Yet, I was considered to be sufficiently capable to continue serving as a sentry.

At this elevation, above the timberline, the weather was unbearable. A steady strong wind blew at all times from Poland, with the effective temperature during nights dropping occasionally to below minus 30 degrees Fahrenheit. The temperature never rose to the freezing point during even a sunny day. It got well below the average daytime temperature at nighttime, especially when the sky was cloudless.

The sentry schedule called for three-hour shifts. To prevent us from freezing to death, we were issued two canvas tent sections into which to wrap ourselves. A makeshift wood stand was placed at critical posts to prevent getting our feet frozen to the ground. After a week of drawing two daily three-hour sentry shifts I was completely exhausted and, from a military standpoint, useless.

The only relief from this ordeal was the view from the top of the bald mountain. On a starry night, one could occasionally see in the east flashes of artillery fire that signaled that the liberators were approaching. I distinctly remember the night when I discovered that. It was shortly after midnight on January 1, 1945. I alarmed the officer on duty, who told me that I must learn how to identify still faraway artillery fire. So far as I was concerned, it was not close enough to suit me.

Three weeks later, when I did not return to the bunker at about 3 a.m. to wake up my relief sentry, the officer on duty went out to check what happened. I was told that I was found on the ground clutching my rifle. That morning a court martial was convened, which would have a perfectly predictable outcome in case the presiding officer found me to have fallen asleep on sentry duty. The execution pit was only a short distance down the slope from the HQ bunker.

Meanwhile the Jewish doctors who were taking care of senior Soviet officers signed a note certifying that I had been unfit to stand on sentry duty for several weeks and that I blacked out from hypothermia, which made me technically a casualty. The commissar who presided over the court martial, the softly speaking redhead Ivanov who knew me from my Batko days, decided to use this occasion to reprimand the officer in charge of the guards for assigning a useless invalid to exceptionally severe sentry duty. The best that Ivanov had to offer was the mildest verdict then available according to the partizan rules. I had to leave the camp.

At the time, the orders to leave the encampment did not look to me much better than a deferred way of perishing. I was ordered to go alone, on a long trek through deep snow, to what was then considered to be a relatively safe mountain village, Liptovska Lužna. I was to seek out an innkeeper who would perhaps arrange for my rest and food. Later I was told that Ivanov took mercy on me in view of the commendation he had awarded the Batko team months before. Without knowing about it, I had been scheduled for a decoration that meanwhile got lost somewhere.

My three weeks in Liptovska Lužna were spent almost entirely sleeping. Upon my arrival in this village, a poor woodcutter named Valent Serafin took me in. During the first few days, as I was teetering on collapse, Valent and his wife took care of me and fed me mashed potatoes as well as a local variety of cottage cheese. After that, I was shuttled from house to house, usually ending up in spaces where the peasants kept their animals. I particularly remember a very kind man, by name of Knobloch, who was an American Slovak and who came to this strictly Catholic village prior to the war as a Baptist missionary. He arranged for me to stay for a few days in a house that was run by a Baptist family of weavers. I hallucinated much of the time, but meanwhile my persistent fever and the festering sores on my feet became tolerable.

When I was leaving Czechoslovakia early in February of 1948, I could not take with me any Czechoslovak currency. From the post office in Prague I mailed Valent a postal check for all the money I had left after receiving my share from the sale of some of my father's properties. In those days, that would be a huge amount. After communications with Czechoslovakia finally reopened forty years later, I tried to reach Valent. I was told that he ended up in the early 1950s working in the Czech uranium mines where he was employed making the timber scaffolding for support of the mining shafts. He did not live long after that. Nobody in the uranium mines did.

Liberation

The military situation in Slovakia in the first weeks of March of 1945 was muddled. War was waged in valleys that could be easily defended by relatively few retreating German troops. The defenders were dug into prepared positions from where they could inflict heavy casualties. The Russian attacks through the Slovak mountains turned out to be much slower than what we were originally promised. Here and there the Russians used the partizans for attacks on the Germans' rear positions but that made no difference. The main thrust of the Russian attack was directed away from the Slovak mountains into the Hungarian plains where their tank armies were making good progress.

Following the incident in which I came to the defense of an innkeeper who had helped me out, I was ordered to leave Liptovska Lužna. I was still in no shape to make the hike back up to the Prašiva mountain. The nearest partizan encampment was only a few miles away, at the end of a passable trail, in the settlement of Železno, which used to be a sanatorium and a spa. When I showed up, I discovered that it was run under the command of a regular Slovak army major who had the unbelievable real name Vražda (meaning "murder"). The partizan detachment was made up of former Slovak gendarmes and a few ex-army officers who managed to escape deportations to German camps. Everybody was sick and not fit for combat. The rooms in the sanatorium had beds, furniture and running water although there was no heat. We burned the furniture to keep warm. In my view, the entire setting looked better than a royal palace.

My greatest and most pleasant surprise was to find in Železno the two doctors I knew from Prašiva, Luža and Blau. It appears that they also had to leave and take with them a number of sick partizans, which included, I recall, five American fliers who always kept themselves apart from everybody. Meeting the doctors was timely because I started coughing out profuse amounts of blood, which Blau diagnosed as an advanced stage of pleurisy.

In the first week of March 1945, everyone in Železno got marching orders to start moving towards the front, which was now close enough so that at night we could distinguish individual rounds from the approaching cannonade. Staying in Železno was also becoming dangerous as it could become a battleground. The problem was that nobody knew exactly how far we would have to walk to cross the front lines to get to the liberated lands. I was told that Vražda chose a difficult trail that would bypass the valleys where Soviet and Rumanian soldiers were advancing slowly and methodically against German rearguard troops. Most of the time, we would be walking on a logging trail high up along the slopes of the mountainside. The purpose was to avoid getting attacked first by the Germans as we marched east and then again by the Russians mistaking us for enemies as we were coming from the west. We would be avoiding places where war was still in progress and ultimately winding up two months later.

I think that it must have been sometime around March 15 when we started on my last march to the east. That involved climbing up steep mountainsides that were still covered by deep snow. It was now clear that others must have taken our trail before because everywhere there were signs of desolation. We encountered many dead bodies as well as discarded items of clothing. The logging paths we traversed must have been used before by retreating partizans. On the sides were partially decomposed bodies that must have been lying there since the fall.

Sometime in the morning of March 20, 1944, without a shot being fired and without much fuss, our sorry-looking column crossed the lines that now defined what was liberated country. The sentries were lethargic Rumanians who did not pay attention to us. They waved us to proceed over a paved highway to the Soviet military checkpoint.

I realized then that the war was over for me.

Transition

After crossing into the so far liberated parts of Czechoslovakia I was finally free of the oppression that began in 1938.

Walking down a road for the first time in seven months without fear of getting shot at was a feeling I could not get used to. Freedom did not present itself as a sudden wonderful relief from all troubles, as we had imagined. It dawned on me that I did not have the slightest idea what to do next except to get my infected and painful molars pulled in a barbershop that happened to be open in the next village.

It took a few days for our group to be processed by what was obviously an NKVD operation. The Americans did not have to wait. A Czechoslovak army staff car picked them up and ferried them to headquarters. Partizans with proper identification as well as Slovak soldiers still in uniform had to march for another day to a place where buses picked us up for delivery to the recruiting offices of the Czechoslovak army in the town of Poprad.

The army medic who examined me did not spend more than a few minutes before stamping me as unfit for military service on account of "advanced pleurisy." I was in sufficiently bad shape that I was immediately carted to a formerly posh hotel in Tatranska Lomnica, which was converted into a hospital, now filled with wounded soldiers and sick partizans. It was heaven to be sleeping in beds with clean sheets and access to an unlimited supply of bread, jam, sugar and running hot water.

The hotel had recently been abandoned by Nazi officers who left a basement full of ammunition and a cache of brand- new, boxed, shoulder-fired antitank weapons (known as the *panzerfaust*). After a few days, it took me and a band of similarly minded firebrands to assist the hotel custodian in getting rid of the panzerfausts by taking them into the hotel tennis court and firing them into a concrete shed.

As soon as I was sufficiently mobile, I also amused myself by writing several short stories that advocated partizan-type vengeance against Nazis and collaborators. These articles would be then tagged to a news items wall display, which became the principal source of war news in the absence of other media. The local commissar, a Capt. Nicholas Langer complimented me on my bloodthirsty style.

After about two weeks of such bliss, recruiters showed up at the hospital seeking to sign up "politically reliable" ex-partizans for an officer course that would be starting in two days. Although at the time it was not clear to me what this was all about, Langer volunteered me as a suitable prospect that was itching to get back into action before the war could end.

The objective of that school was to send trusted partizans to join the military police that would be given the job of conducting purges in the newly occupied territories. Because I spoke some German I was expected to move to the Sudetenland, the region that was populated by ethnic Germans who were Hitler's pretext for dismembering Czechoslovakia in 1938. There were scores to be settled and I was certainly the type who would do whatever needed to be done, such as "ethnic cleansing." As a sign of the motley collection of characters assembled a few days later this included my bunkmate Jozef Staudinger, who subsequently became one of the judges who sentenced Josef Tiso, the former president of the Slovak state, to hanging.

I never made it to the Sudetenland. The war ended on May 5 and when our advance troops arrived in the borderland, all of the Germans were gone.

At graduation sometime in the second week of May 1945, I was the only member of the class who did not did gain an officer rank because the head of the school found out that I was only sixteen. All I got was the rank of a full corporal in the Czechoslovak Army as well marching orders to leave for Bratislava as bodyguard to a colonel in the military police.

5. On the Way to the Bratislava Posting, May 1945

With my automatic pistol and dressed in an army uniform, I stopped on my way to Trenčín. So far as I knew, my mother would still be hiding somewhere and my sister could still be wandering through the countryside with forged identity papers. When I suddenly showed up at our former home, there was no news about anybody. I found out that my mother and my sister were captured and sent away to Germany. My father and grandparents had been deported.

I halted in Trenčín for only one day and enjoyed how some of my former torturers showed they were afraid. After strutting on the main square for a while in my new uniform, I saw no point in settling any scores. Despite the dreams about retribution I had been nursing for months, I peacefully departed to Bratislava to report to my new army post, as ordered.

I stayed in the army for another three months. I didn't like it because most of my work involved expediting mountains of paperwork and running errands because communications did not work well. There were no purges to conduct because a legal bureaucracy now took over to let just about all perpetrators walk free. Ethnic cleansing was also not necessary since all Germans as well as collaborators had fled to the American-occupied zone of Germany.

My boss in Bratislava was now Col. Nicholas Langer. After appraising the situation he ordered me to get out of the army because there was no career there for a sixteen-year-old Jewish boy without any education.

In the fall of 1945, I returned to Trenčín to share quarters with my sister who had just returned from a slave labor camp. Nobody else from my family came back.

In the fall of 1945, time had finally arrived to resume a normal life, to start organizing for a new existence and to start forgetting about the lost years. My first priority was to obtain a passport to leave the country. It took a great deal of effort, unending paperwork, divestment of all claims on property, a certificate of political reliability and a hefty bribe to finally obtain a passport which would allow me to get out of Czechoslovakia. It took me until October of 1947 to accomplish that.

6. Paul's Passport Picture - 1947

In due course I received the much sought-after papers authenticating my participation in the uprising.

7. Grant for Partizan Badge

This certification became the basis for receiving back pay from the Czechoslovak army for the entire period served.

8. Certification as Czechoslovak Partizan

Sachsenhausen

Sometime in June we received father's only and last communication since he was seized eight months before. The letter was posted April 7[th,] 1945, from Oranienburg, Germany, located near Berlin. He was identified as Israel Adolf Strassmann, #42690, Block 15, Sachsenhausen Camp. The letter was addressed to our neighbor, a Mr. Kišš, a close family friend who had served as our godfather when the family was baptized in 1942.

9. Father's Letter from Sachsenhausen

In his letter Father is inquiring about "Kubinska", where my mother went into hiding.

Judging from his firm handwriting father must have still been in full possession of his faculties. The Sachsenhausen camp was liberated on April 22nd! On April 20th and 21th, 1945, because of the Soviet Army advance, 33,000 prisoners were forced to leave the camp on the Death March. They were divided in groups of 400. The SS intended to embark them on ships and then sink those ships. Thousands of inmates died marching, without food, water or shelter. The SS shot anyone who was too weak to walk. After liberation Soviet soldiers found only 3,000 survivors in the camp. Most of them were starving, ill and too weak to welcome their liberators. Like in several other camps, and despite of the medical cares they received, most inmates died in the following days.

Without Father there was nothing to keep me any more in Slovakia. I had to leave to start a new life somewhere where I would not be haunted daily by the people and the locations that would keep reminding me about the experiences of the recent years. If I could go to America I could perhaps close an epoch of my life that I still keep calling "my war."

Part II
Family

Origins

I was born in Trenčín, Czechoslovakia and much of my story revolves about life and experiences in and around that town until I left it forever ten days before the communist takeover in 1948.

In the 1930s, it was a town of about 11,000. It was nestled against a huge fortress that was built on top of a protruding cliff that rose over a narrow valley carved out by the river Váh. It was the defensible passage from the Carpathian Mountains before the valley spread into the vast Danube plain in the south.

Since early in the twelfth century, the town had been the district capital from which the surrounding villages obtained manufactured goods, medical services, resolution of legal matters as well as interference from whatever government was in power during frequent changes in the controlling regimes. The fortunes of the Strassmann family were derived from this setting where commerce had always flourished.

Early in its history Trenčín, thanks to its geographic and strategic location in the valley, became one of the key towns from where Slovakia was governed. Archaeological findings have proved settlement as early as 2000 BC. When the Romans moved the borders of their empire to the river Danube, they constructed several fortified camps as warning outposts that would be guarding invasion passages through the Carpathian Mountains. Trenčín has proof of Roman presence in the form of an inscription on the castle rock that commemorates victory of the emperor Marcus Aurelius (AD 161–180). As a child, I was fascinated by this and began developing an early interest in history from the many monuments surrounding me.

In the era of prosperity of the Great Moravian Empire, Trenčín belonged to the Nitra Principality. This region became a part of Hungary in the first half of eleventh century. Trenčín became a seat of the border district administration and later the center of the royal district. After the invasion by the Turks in thirteenth century, it was devastated. In 1275, the newly constructed castle became property of the magnate Peter Čák. Trenčín was finally raised by the King Zigmund to become a free royal town in 1412. It could then grant charters to guilds that formed the basis for the rise of merchants and craftsmen. For instance, as late as in 1890, with the town's population of 5,100, there were 174 shoemakers (cobblers) and 106 tailors.

10. The Trenčin Castle (1998). B = Paul's Birthplace

The walled town nestled against the fortress dates back perhaps to the eighth century and protected its citizens against brigands and raiders, thus creating a reasonably secure community in which Jewish merchants found a tolerable existence perhaps as far back as the fifteenth century.

Political Instability

Perhaps more than in other European towns, the history of Trenčín is one of disasters, wars and oppressive occupations by whoever was the winner at the time. The town had to resist frequent invasions from the Turks who rampaged through the countryside, looting villages, but never succeeding in conquering the city itself. The town experienced much damage at the time of the Kuruc (Cross Bearers) peasant rebellion in 1680. The castle was burned down at the end of the eighteenth century when it could not defend itself any more against artillery attacks.

The evidence of political instability was everywhere and formed a deep imprint on how the peasantry and the town folks behaved whenever rulers changed. Fortunes were either destroyed or transferred through expropriation whenever a new government assumed power. For instance, the peasantry benefited from what was labeled as "land reform" when the new Czechoslovak government took over in 1919. When the Slovak Republic was created in 1938, property was distributed to party faithful and again in 1942 when Jewish assets were taken over. This pattern was continued in 1945 with the confiscation of property acquired by the Nazi collaborators, in 1948 with the nationalization of everything by the communists, and again in 1998 with the disintegration of the Soviet regime, and when Czechoslovakia broke up into separate Czech and Slovak nations.

SHAPING A CONSCIOUSNESS

My childhood was formed through encounters with the ghosts of the past. On the street leading to the castle was a house that had been the living quarters of the local executioner until the start of the nineteenth century. On the way to the river, I passed old ramparts where "witches" were burned as recently as late as 1760. My elementary school was constructed so that one of the corridors leaned against the walls surrounding the fortress. At the gates of the town one could find walls where cannonballs were still embedded. Our favorite playgrounds were on the grounds of the castle where we climbed through abandoned dungeons and where old objects could be unearthed occasionally.

Industrialization commenced early in the nineteenth century with investments from French textile firms seeking cheap labor. Trenčín became a trade and industrial center in the second half of nineteenth century. The establishment of many industrial enterprises and financial institutions as well as a railway connection to Žilina on the way to Poland, across the Carpathian Mountains, contributed to an economic boom in the manufacture of clothing and foodstuff.

Although the awareness of most of the Jewish youths in Eastern Europe was formed in largely agricultural surroundings and was dominated by religious life, my own experiences reflected exposures to industrialized, military, secular and commercial forms.

The center of the town, or the "old town," was inside a walled enclave that surrounded the property owners' houses as late as the sixteenth century. Walls separated the town from the fortifications of the castle. My grandfather's house was one of the prominent homes facing the central square. Extending further out from the walled main square were streets that reflected the growth of the population, with the most desirable location for stores located where my father started his business in 1919 and then relocated to a new building in 1934.

Trenčín was a prized medieval possession for any regime. Its trade, guilds and services generated good tax revenues for the rulers and a tolerable level of prosperity for its citizens, who enjoyed municipal liberties as was customary in the medieval times for those who had citizen privileges. In due course such traditions were extended also to Jewish traders and professionals, which made the town an attractive location where to settle.

During my youth, the pervasive military presence was a prominent feature. Because of its location Trenčín had always had a military garrison as far back as historical records could show. Two large military complexes were located at each end of the town. In the surrounding fields there were remnants of ammunition storage depots. Across the river was a mock battlefield, with trenches, bunkers and machine gun emplacements that were used in training exercises. One could not avoid observing daily army drills on the large pastureland only a few hundred yards from the center of the town. I was always late for my piano lessons because I halted to observe through an open iron fence what was going on at the grounds of the local 71st Company. One of my close friends was the son of a major in the 71st.

The local sense of history, persistence of violence and military presence became a forming influence shaping my awareness in ways I could not predict as preparedness for the approaching hardships.

Family

I was born on one of the coldest days over a century in a country where the winters were always severe, on January 24, 1929, in Trenčín.

11. Birthplace, Grandfather Strassmann's House

This ancient town was formerly part of Hungary, later Austro-Hungary, subsequently split into the Czechoslovak Republic, then separated into the Slovak state, after war restructured as Czecho-Slovakia and currently the Slovak Republic. All that happened, in that order of succession, in less than a century. My political senses were sharpened by the fact that I had the experience of living under three different regimes and had been subjected to three different military commands.

FATHER

My father was born in 1894 in Horny Lideč, which is a small village in Moravia not too far from Trenčín. He was murdered in Germany at the age of forty-one sometime in April 1945.

My father Adolf was a physically vigorous, stern, independent-minded and decisive former military man. He was thirty-one years old when I was born. My mother and friends called him Adko, but in affectionate moments Mother called him Joni. Since I inherited his freethinking streak I was often disciplined. I was always inclined to experiment to see how far I could push any of the many rules beyond their limits.

Father graduated from a commerce academy in Vienna, which was an exceptionally high level of achievement in those days. One of my father's many admirable traits was his penmanship. All of his ledger entries were made in precise and organized manuscript. In those days, penmanship and clarity in record keeping were among the requirements for holding a trusted position.

On account of his education and because of his already recognized sense of leadership he became a commissioned officer in the local regiment of the Austro-Hungarian army at the start of the World War in 1914. He served with distinction in Russia, in Bosnia and in Italy.

12. Father on his Favorite Black Horse, Zigany, in Bosnia

He left the service as a major in a combat command, which was most unusual for a Jewish man. During the campaign in Italy he was wounded from a close artillery hit. Not all of the shrapnel was removed and I recall that it was not until sometime in 1936 when a remaining piece of metal worked itself out of his calf where it could be surgically removed. His many medals, plus the just removed shrapnel, were in a box that was in a bedroom drawer right next to my mother's preferred cologne, #4711.

After Father returned from the war in 1918, he established a modest retail food shop.

13. Father in the early 1920s

Subsequently he expanded it into what ultimately became a flourishing wholesale food and agricultural products business. He grew the business rapidly during the 1930s, during the relative prosperity of the Czechoslovak republic despite the economic depression elsewhere in Europe. Father became one of the dominant merchants in the Trenčín district, with two diesel trucks delivering merchandise to retail stores located throughout the surrounding villages.

As a child I vividly remember the daily routine that started before 6 AM, in summer or in winter, with the filling of orders, staging them in the yard for pickup by a crew that would then proceed loading the goods into trucks or wagons (many horse drawn) for delivery. Another memory is the smell of roast coffee. We roasted a fresh twenty-kilo batch of coffee on a hand-turned wood-burning stove every other day. At least once a week, the stove was converted to roasting peanuts (known locally as "American nuts"). Often I ended up turning the handle of the roasting drum and every so often inserting a sampler through the axle to see if the coffee was of the right dark brown color. When the coffee was done it was dumped onto a large copper screen and quenched with a bucket of water.

My parents worked with intense diligence. After they supervised loading the trucks the business was open to the retail trade until noon. The store then closed down for a lunch siesta and re-opened at 3 PM., staying open until as late as 9 PM. Those were the store hours six days a week, plus a half-day on Sundays when the peasants from the neighboring towns came to offer produce on the marketplace and then proceeded to shop from local stores. The most efficient way in which this could work out was for the family to live in an apartment one floor above the store.

FATHER'S WAR

My father went into the First World War as the commanding officer of a local unit. During the years of great hardships he created close ties with men who were his noncommissioned officers, who had been drafted from the surrounding villages. I understood that my father was respected enormously because he always tried to save the lives of the troops by avoiding head-on bayonet charges against machine guns, which were the military tactics dictated by Austrian generals.

I believe that much of the commercial success of my father could be traced to his continued relationships with his erstwhile veterans, many now advancing themselves as storekeepers in the neighboring villages. Father knew who could be trusted for an extension of credit. That was the principal reason why successful local distributors of agricultural products were switching their business to our wholesale firm.

I do not think that the modern military has a full appreciation of the way the military was organized in the Austro-Hungarian Empire. The conscription was almost entirely from local villages. The companies were named after the town from whence they came. Individual units were designated by the name of the commanding officer. In those days the commanding officer had enormous powers, receiving from the army only uniforms, weapons, ammunition and cash. Food, medical care and transport were usually sequestered from local villages, especially as the war progressed and military logistics became unreliable. In many respects the customs and behavior of such a military organization were not much advanced over the medieval practice of each unit looking out for their maximum self-sufficiency and minimum casualties. In this way each unit was dependent on its wellbeing and survival on the quality of the leadership of their commanding officers.

MOTHER

My mother was an independently strong but very even-tempered lady, born in Budapest in 1904. She was twenty-five when I was born. I was the second child, preceded by my sister Ella, born in 1925. My mother Frances, or Františka (everybody called her Franci) came from a family of craftsmen and not from traders like most of the Jews. She had a reputation as a practical, honest and caring friend. My father married my mother in 1924. The wedding was at the Scheibner Hotel, then the only kosher hotel in town.

14. Parents' Wedding Picture – 1924

My mother was a beautiful, hardworking woman. She was a full partner with my father in business affairs, sharing the heavy burdens of building a business while keeping long hours to manage our household.

She was the cashier and peacemaker in the store and in our extended family. Our business had a dozen employees who did not always get along.

15. Mother as a Young Girl

My sister, who spent the last days with my mother in Ravensbruck, said that my mother's only regrets about her life was that she did not spend as much time with us children as she had wished. My mother used to call me *spaček*, the Slovak diminutive for the starling bird that was known as daring, curious, and a nuisance. This was certainly a good characterization of my childhood behavior. I was frequently punished for all sorts of trespasses, including an inclination to experiment with forbidden things and organizing elaborate pranks.

After 1940 my mother had to leave her position in business and tend to the household, taking over from the formerly employed nurse and a cook. The staff was dismissed when our housing was squeezed into only two rooms. I got to see the most of my mother only when the troubled times arrived, even though everyday distractions, including the hunt for food supplies, diverted most of her attention. It was remarkable in those days that somehow our household always had plenty to eat, including fruits and vegetables. Mother's gentile friends made sure that she received a supply of whatever was the latest crop. With limited refrigeration capacity most of the fruit was stored on top of the dresser in the parents' bedroom. We could eat the fruit only when brown spots started to appear on the skin. Nevertheless, there was always a surplus for making food packages with canned goods and smoked sausages to send to concentration camps. It was my job to make the packages and bring them to the post office.

FAMILY LIFE

My parents were avid hikers. I still have many pictures that were taken in the early 1930s in the Tatra mountains, which were Father's favorite vacation place. The last few family pictures were taken on the terrace near the children's bedrooms prior to the eviction from our own house. As conditions worsened the terrace offered the only place where we could gather for a few moments in peace.

16. Parents' Last Picture Together – 1941

The earliest that I remember of my childhood experiences were the rituals of the family that revolved around Jewish holidays. The peak holiday was of course Passover. It triggered a hyperactive fuss supervised by my mother because all dishes had to be exchanged for another set. All sorts of preparations took place that had to conform to the prescribed rituals, which included a carp in aspic and a roast goose. I always ran errands for my mother to help her out. Perhaps as early as the age of seven I learned how to pull the dough to make thin dough for strudel pastry, or knead flour, yeast, sugar and butter to make dumplings.

My father gave the appearance that he was modestly religious, but I always suspected that he was a crypto-agnostic. Mother insisted on keeping a kosher household, much of that on account of respect for my grandfather Alexander who lived with us. We separated in our kitchen the *fleishig* (meat) dishes and utensils for serving meals from the *milchig* (dairy) dishes and utensils for meals that would be touching any milk products. In the attic we stored another set of dishes that were used to replace every single kitchen item during Passover holidays. Adherence to a kosher kitchen was a great burden and therefore we employed additional help before and during the holidays. All of the dishes had to be carefully washed in separate batches to conform to ritual procedures. Just consider the burdens this imposed on my mother. Our kitchen was equipped with a wood-burning stove and only cold running water. For dishwashing, we had to heat water in a huge pot. The pot had to be hit with a hammer to break off the steadily accumulating layers of calcium deposits formed from the city water supply.

The household was labor intensive. I still do not understand how my mother could manage the cooking and washing while taking care of business and family affairs. I remember that the job of washing my sister's hair was always a big affair because Mother insisted using only water that was calcium-free and soap that did not leave foam precipitates on my sister's raven-black hair. For that purpose we kept a barrel to accumulate rainwater cascading from the tiled roof of the house. Hair was washed when there was a sufficient accumulation of fresh rainwater.

17. Ella and Paul, Always Together, Sometime in 1937

Even through we were considered to be one of the most prosperous Jewish families in town and lived in a modern house built in 1934, we still depended on cold running water throughout the house. The most modern feature of our house was the central steam heating for the living quarters. That worked just fine but occasionally it generated burbling noises when the steam condensed faster than the heat that came up from the basement three levels below the living quarters. To heat the house we burned anthracite coal, which was delivered once a year and required an elaborate fire-starting routine on a cold morning. Only the main bathroom had hot running water and even then only when the wood-burning copper stove in the bathroom was lit. For that I had to carry wood three stories up from the basement every Friday, which was set as the mandatory bathing schedule. We also had a wood-burning stove in the attic for heating water for the weekly washing of linens. That offered another flight of stairs for delivering the wood.

Mother insisted that I bathe only in water that did not leave a calcium deposit or soap residue anywhere on my body. Additional scrubbing as well as an elaborate rinsing procedure always followed a bath. The bathing sequence always ended by cutting and shaping of toenails and fingernails.

SISTER

I have an older sister, Ella, the only survivor from the family. She still lives in Trenčín. She never left that town except for the time she spent in the Ravensbruck labor camp in 1944 and 1945.

Ella inherited all of my mother's best characteristics. She has always been helpful, hard working and considerate of others. It was my sister who first brought me into Hashomer-Hatzair (the Young Guards) and who always warned me to behave myself as I was on the verge of getting discovered as the source of trouble. Otherwise, our lives were separate even though we shared a tiny bedroom for several years and it was she who always tidied the mess I left. I became particularly jealous of her when she reached the age of seventeen and several young men started courting her. I particularly remember pranks to discourage them, such as sending

Gejza Fabian, her future husband, on false errands. He seemed to me as being too much likely as a prospective groom.

18. My Dearest Sister Ella, 1940

During the war, Ella kept herself very much apart from me. She maintained her connections with young Jewish men and women, many now hiding with false identity papers, but who still needed ways to contact sources of money. Ella was strictly forbidden to engage in such activities, especially in cases where she would act as a courier. I suspect that in her quiet and unassuming ways she must have fooled everybody by continuing such missions. Besides, after 1942, I could attend school and would be spending much time with my Lutheran friends, whereas she had a very boring clerical job.

When she was betrayed sometime in October 1944, she was shipped first to the Sered concentration camp and then to Germany. Her life was preserved by getting assigned as a slave laborer to a factory where salvaged parts from downed Luftwaffe airplanes were cleaned for subsequent reuse as spare parts. Without any protective clothing or gloves, the Jewish girls had to see to it that metal components were cleaned with corrosive solvents.

As the Soviet army approached from the east, the slave laborers from her factory were ordered to evacuate and to start marching west what became known as the "death march." By this time Ella was starved and so sick it would be only a matter of time before she would have to rest and then face inevitable death meted out to all stragglers. She was saved by two of her childhood friends who shared a potato with her and propped her up when her feet buckled.

In the last days of the war, her marching column was sufficiently dispersed that when she and her friends heard the approaching artillery bombardment, they found a way of drifting from others while passing through a forest. They somehow managed to survive in the woods for a few days until liberation.

Ella returned to Trenčín, where she discovered I was alive. After that, she tried her best to set up a home for both of us, but my intentions were already drifting away from Slovakia to life in America. Ella married her teen-age sweetheart, Gejza, and bore two children who are now physicians. There are four grandchildren.

Her suffering did not end. Under the communist regime she was reduced to holding a lowly clerical position and was exposed to all of the deprivations meted out by a police state. She has somehow learned to cope with the hardships of the years by preserving a sharp mind, a friendly attitude for everyone and a stoic disposition. When we talk about sorrows, past or present, she always finishes the conversation with the phrase "you cannot do much about that."

She has always remained my dearest friend, to this day.

Grandfather Strassmann

Father was the son of an innkeeper, Filip Strassmann, who invested whatever money he could into my father's education. I do not remember much of him since he always kept himself aloof on account of his heart condition (angina pectoris, so far as I can recall because he kept popping nitroglycerin pills). Grandfather smoked an old-fashioned pipe with a long stem that dangled down to his belt and smelled awfully.

Filip had two brothers and one sister younger than him. His original domicile was in the village of Strelnica, which is located at the border between Slovakia and Bohemia. For many years he lived in Horny Lideč where he worked on a nobleman's estate as administrative manager as well as owner of a local inn. He moved to Trenčín before the start of the First

World War, where he acquired another inn in what was then the poorest district of Trenčín known as Alsovaros.

Grandmother Anna was born in Beluša, where, until their deportation in 1942 lived her brother with a large family. Anna's brother, Ziegler, had four sons and a daughter. Three of the Zieglers survived. One fled early in 1939 to England and fought in the English army, another obtained false documents and survived without being identified as a Jew throughout the war. How the third Ziegler, Ferdinand, survived nobody knows except that he suddenly appeared in Poprad in eastern Slovakia in March of 1945 as political officer of the Czechoslovak army that came from the Soviet Union.

One of the Ziegler sisters, Hanna, married, against the will of her parents, a gentile farmer in the nearby village. She survived the war unmolested and died peacefully in 1946. Grandmother Anna as well as the entire Ziegler family never spoke of her or saw her since she married a gentile peasant. That was considered a great shame for a Jewish family. My sister found about this family secret only by accident many years after Hanna was not alive any more.

It appears that Grandfather Filip's prosperity during the First World War allowed him to accumulate sufficient wealth to purchase a prominent house on the main square in the center of the town where I was born. To this date, this house is still owned by my sister Ella and by her two children, Dr. Thomas (Tommy) Fabian and Dr. Zuzka (Susan) Eckmannova.

I think that Grandfather Filip was able to become relatively well-to-do by exercising an uncommon level of frugality, such as hand-delivering all mail to save on postage. I was told that he once walked, during an especially hard winter, over fifty miles to return money owed. Whereas my penniless carpenter grandfather Weiner always treated me to some special sweets (from the local Turkish hawker) every Saturday after the prayers, I do not recall ever having received any presents from Grandfather Filip, although Grandmother Anna treated me always to well-baked potato skins with fried onions (to this date my favorite meal).

My paternal grandmother, Anna (also called *malka* because she was small), born Ziegler, came from a large clan which included us in a large circle of relatives who were always visiting us or us visiting them.

Some of them came to live with us or near us when they were dispossessed in 1940. After the deportations started in 1942 my father could not protect them anymore and they all perished, including my mechanical genius Uncle Kling who taught me how to repair electrical outlets and fuses that had frequently shorted out.

During the period from 1942 through September 1944 my paternal grandparents were protected by my father's "presidential exception," also known as the "white card." Early in September 1944 my grandparents were deported to Oswiecim where they perished.

Grandfather Weiner

By far my most favorite member of the family was my maternal grandfather Alexander (Dedko) Weiner. He spent more time with me than anyone else in the family, especially after the outside world closed in on us after 1938. He was one of the few Jewish craftsmen who made very fine cabinetry, usually inlaid with veneer made of rare woods. Orders for such furniture were often placed years ahead of delivery, frequently to become available as a girl's dowry. That timing was quite predictable because it was considered a shame if a girl was not engaged to be married before she turned twenty.

Dedko had an optimistic outlook on life. He was known as the only person who said, "It could be worse," whenever someone brought bad news, which was an increasingly frequent occurrence. He liked to sing or hum Yiddish songs when he worked. He closed down his shop sometime in 1935 and moved in with us, occupying a tiny room in the attic of our house and taking on the thankless job as yard supervisor to make sure that merchandise was not stolen. He also saw to it that I attended prayers every Saturday and all major holidays without any excuses. Together we used to visit the carpentry shop of his former apprentice, Molnar, where Dedko supervised the delicate process of applying layers of varnish to fine woods. Since the smell of turpentine and lacquer was strong, Dedko and Molnar used to help themselves to ample doses of 100%-proof plum brandy "to counter the vapors."

After 1940, when our ability to walk in the streets was restricted (there were elaborate regulations limiting the time and streets where we would be allowed to appear) Dedko set up in his tiny room a small workshop to teach me the art of making fine veneer inlays. We started making small wooden boxes for jewelry. To this day I appreciate the enormous amount of labor that craftsmen must invest in making artifacts that involve inlays of stone or wood.

Grandfather's reputation as a master cabinetmaker temporarily saved him from deportation to an annihilation camp in 1942. Instead he was sent to a slave labor camp in Nováky operated by the Slovak fascists as a business enterprise for the benefit of the top-ranking Guard officials. One of the specialties of this camp was the manufacture of custom furniture. I was told by one of the surviving inmates that Dedko was admired for his cheerful disposition and conviction that a liberating messiah may miraculously appear any moment. Dedko had the reputation of always looking for some good when everyone was despondent. I am sure he went to his death with expectations of relief from all the woes of this earth. I will always think about my grandfather's saying "it could be worse" when somebody brings me bad news.

GRANDMOTHER WEINER

I do not recall much about my maternal grandmother Emma (born Diamant) except that when I was about three years old I came to visit her while she was resting in bed. She was very pale and the visit was short. I was told that this would be the last time I would see her. Emma was much respected as a wise woman. She had a tiny store selling embroidery patterns at one of the best locations in town. My grandmother not only sold the patterns but also coached the girls how to improve the quality and complexity of their embroidery.

19. Grandmother Emma Weiner

Her additional income came from being a much- respected marriage broker. How this came about offers an interesting insight into the Jewish community life of her era. As in all societies, birth, marriage and burial were the decisive events for every family. Of these, marriage was perhaps most important, because it involved an element of choice in an environment largely constrained by custom and economics. Picking the right marriage partner was often a key to a family's rise in status and frequently also to prosperity. Dowries and inheritance played an important role in property matters. For a girl to be married to the right family was decisive. It was often one of the principal topics of chitchat in the synagogue or the coffeehouse.

To prepare for marriage and as part of the social pressure on the girl to follow traditional patterns of behavior she had to start making her trousseau as soon as she entered school. That involved learning needlework and embroidery almost totally based on patterns sold in one of the many handicraft shops in town. I do not think that my grandmother Emma's shop was much bigger than a hundred square feet, but it was filled with wooden trays carrying then-fashionable copper metal patterns embedded into them. The mother of a girl brought in a piece of linen upon which my grandmother then embossed the pattern in washable blue ink. After practicing on scraps of linens as a sampler of the various stitches, the girl received approval from Emma to continue working on her trousseau, first doing simple borders for bedsheets and pillowcases. In due course the girl was allowed to work on showpiece tablecloths.

As the story goes, my grandmother was very much in love with my grandfather Alexander. During the First World War, Emma stayed alone in Budapest. She was there when the news was brought to her that her husband was killed, which of course was not true. She went into a severe shock and subsequently suffered from a weakened heart condition, finally passing away in 1932.

THE EMMA IQ TEST

During all of this time, consuming untold hundreds of hours, girls continued to be under the watchful eye of Emma to produce works of increasing complexity depending on intelligence, pattern-recognition skills and industriousness. Observing how a little girl matured into marriageable age through her work offered perhaps as good a prediction about the girl's desirable characteristics as any aptitude test that could be then available. Emma's word was frequently decisive when marriage contracts were negotiated and the relative merits of the candidate brides were compared.

Of course, my grandmother made sure that her only daughter Frances was suitably coached as the most attractive prospect for perhaps the most desirable suitor then available in town. That was my father, a former company commander and one of the few Jews with higher education. I do not know any of the details about how the marriage was planned, although I doubt very much that my father could have been talked into anything he had not decided to do anyway.

Years later, two women from Trenčín told me they could have been my mother had it not been for the unfair advantage created by that "schemer from the embroidery shop." My sister Ella vehemently denies this story, yet I find it a plausible explanation for why the two more assertive (rich, but not too bright) women did not have much of a chance, despite their claims.

The emphasis the Jewish communities placed on choices in which learning and intelligence were considered more important than wealth offers a partial explanation for the propensity of Jews to favor intellectual pursuits. Tradition often dictated that a learned, even if poor, Jewish young man was preferred as a husband for a girl from a good family. That made many families a matriarchy. It did not take me much time to figure that out when I married, completely penniless, into the prominent Rosenthal matriarchy (of the Maidenform bra manufacturing fame) in 1954. The entire clan showed up for the wedding and was visibly delighted to see one of their grandnieces marry a poor but promising European import.

THE STRASSMANN BUSINESS

The evidence of my father's rapid success in business was the house completed during the economic depression in 1934. It was made of reinforced concrete. It was a centrally steam-heated home, which included offices, the shipping yard, the warehouses and the family apartment. An architect, who found it difficult to supervise contractors, finally completed it after much delay and ample help from Father. The building inspectors were also not accustomed to a modern design that combined both living and business uses. The architect for the structure was a certain Silberstein who was supposed to enjoy a high reputation for designing public buildings. He also designed the totally custom-made cabinetry for our dining and living rooms. Some is still in excellent shape as components of the furniture were salvaged by my sister and in use in her small one-bedroom apartment in Trenčín.

A special characteristic of the construction was the flat roof on top of the warehouse. The roof was covered with about one foot of topsoil on which we grew strawberries, flowers and some shrubs. There was also a small grass lawn on which one could rest to get a suntan, or to build a fortress-like tent out of blankets which became my favorite plaything during early childhood.

Facing the street was our apartment consisting of a dining room, a living room (which was hardly ever used) and the parents' bedroom. The two children's bedrooms faced the terrace. The kitchen and the cook's quarters faced the yard. The roofline was 45 feet above the street level; the length of the house was 135 feet and the entire structure occupied an entire building block. In the 1960s the house was razed to make way for a theater and entertainment center serving the Slovak Army. It is now used for concerts and other public events.

20. Business Storefront. Family Apartment Upstairs.

The display on the storefront used to announce that the Strassmann firm was engaged in a "Business with Diversified Merchandise in Retail and Wholesale, Fertilizer, Feed and Agricultural Supplies." Next to the store was a large gate through which trucks and the farmers' carts entered into the yard for loading. On the ground floor was room for another store that was rented out as a contribution to mortgage payments. Right next to the store entrance was a steel door opening into the basement for unloading of goods that needed cool and dry storage.

Father's rise as a leading merchant in the district can be traced to his innovation in financing his distribution channels, thus ending up with the establishment of a retail distribution chain which was headed in each of these villages by a war veteran he knew he could trust. He expanded these relationships by including the distribution of kerosene to local villages. The Strassmann firm became the regional agents for the American firm Standard Oil of New York. Perhaps as many as a hundred steel-rimmed barrels of this highly inflammable stuff were kept in the basement underneath the warehouse, just a few yards from our bedrooms.

Father also introduced to the district the use of high-nitrate fertilizer to increase agricultural yields. Sometimes there was enough nitrate of ammonia stacked up in the yard to blow up the neighborhood. Our firm also imported high-quality flour from the USA in varieties that were not available from local mills. I recall that we were able to supply local house-wives with the much-sought-after semolina flour from Nebraska.

In a period of twenty years he and my mother (the treasurer, cashier and personnel relations manager) managed to build up a business, that flourished and expanded steadily until 1938. I believe that my father was able to succeed because of his commercial education, whereas his primary competitors (the Fursts who had the business for more than a century) were just relaxing and not innovating. My father's prosperity was largely driven by the pleasures he got from risky commercial innovations. For some reason I still remember the stories I heard about my father trying to corner the local market for a vastly popular product made out of prunes that were used to sweeten one of the mainstays of the peasant diet, which were steamed dumplings. Every fall, my father bought from Bosnia a car-load of prunes at exceptionally low prices, and. for one reason or another, there was always something wrong with this merchandise that allowed my mother to always remark that bargains do not pay off.

Because of my father's concentration on business and on enhanc-ing the commercial affairs in the district he was respected as one of the leading citizens in town. As a matter of fact, he was the first Jew elected to the district council. That was a regulatory commission that governed the commercial and other local regulations that remained under the control of the town government under grants of privileges dating back for centu-ries. After the war, without any commercial experience, I was granted full membership in the local merchant councils based solely on my father's prior position in that body.

I remember that many of the local merchants resented Father's re-served streak for not visiting the local coffeehouses. These were the favor-ite gathering places for the local dealmakers and for gossips. Years later I was reminded that I was just like my father in my walking habits, always walking faster than anyone thought proper in a conservative society that did not favor changes.

I think that my father's outlook was much more cosmopolitan than that of other merchants, whether Jewish or not. The sign on our store in-cluded the phrase "Merchants in Colonial Wares" which included a variety of imported goods. Our store carried camphor from India (for homemade remedies to cure colds), tea from Ceylon, cloves from Java (of ceremonial use during Jewish and Catholic holidays), cinnamon from Madagascar, sardines from Portugal, semolina flour from Nebraska, kerosene from Baku at the Caspian Sea, ammonia fertilizer from Chile and coffee from Brazil. In today's supermarkets such riches and variety are commonplace. In a small provincial town in Czechoslovakia in the middle of the economic depression of the 1930s such variety was remarkable.

One of Father's great experiences was his one visit to London and Brussels sometime in the early 1930s. I remember that our library at home was filled with travelogues, including the complete works of Sven Hedin, the explorer who wrote about central Asia and particularly about Tibet. My father's dream of supreme accomplishment was to own a large garden, somewhere in a land of peace and tolerance, which to him always meant England. In such a setting his children and grandchildren would be attending the best international universities and speak English.

As I look out now on the meadow in front of my computer screen where I wrote this book, I often think that this is exactly what my father would have sought as a life that is as good as it can get when seen from the perspective of existence in Trenčín, just before the bad times began.

RELATIVES

I was always aware that relatives were important because much of the life and conversation revolved about their lives and troubles, of which there was always plenty, especially as their dependency on my father grew. They were certainly a colorful lot.

Though Jews were generally not engaged in the engineering profession, I developed during my childhood the fixed idea that this was what I wished to be. There was cousin Karol Schalk, who was completing his studies in mechanical engineering in Prague. There were also vague references to the eastern branch of the Strassmann family where a Moritz Strassmann held the position as supervisory engineer on the staff of the Hungarian Railroad. Many years later I obtained from his nephew a medal that was given to Moritz for his services in the construction of a number of railroad tunnels between Hungary and the Ukraine.

Perhaps the most colorful Strassmann relative was Erwin Soos, whom I discovered after the war when I located him in Aachen, Germany. According to Erwin, his mother was a sister of Moritz Strassmann. Against the opposition of all relatives she married Soos's father, who was then the political commissar of the abortive Kuhn communist revolt in 1918. Soos's father was executed when the uprising failed. A monument to him was erected after 1945 in Košice.

Soos, a devoted lifetime communist, subsequently served as editor of one of the leading Slovak communist newspapers and became head of the Czechoslovak foreign broadcasting news services. In one of the many Soviet purges Soos was imprisoned, but on account of his family's long service to communism, was allowed to go into voluntary exile to Germany, where he eked out the remaining few years of his life in great bitterness. In addition to receiving a small pension from the German government, as a former slave laborer, he supported himself by analyzing the contents of several dozen communist-regime newspapers for the Oxford Analytica publishers. During the Cold War his work became a useful source of much information for the western intelligence services. Such work was always done by émigrés who had a good understanding of how to interpret the meager sources of news as it was leaking from behind the Iron Curtain.

Life

It is alleged in some historical summaries that Jewish merchants were present in Trenčín at the end of the second century A.D. when it was a Roman camp and Jews were intermediaries in the trade between Romans and Germanic tribes. Trenčín was on a key road passing through what is now the last narrow gap in the mountain ranges between the Polish and Hungarian plains.

In 1938 about 89,000 Jews lived in Slovakia. Some 10,000 lived in the territory subsequently ceded to Hungary (in Ruthenia and sub-Carpathia) in 1940, leaving about 79,000 Jews making up 3 percent of the population. Slovakia was poorer and far less industrialized than the historic Czech crown provinces of Bohemia and Moravia, and so were its Jews. They were engaged mostly in retail trade. A small number of Jews provided a large share of legal and medical services.

The Jewish Community

There are no records about Jewish communities except for a mention of a trading group in Komarno in the eleventh century about 70 kilometers to the south. There was a large influx of Jews into Slovakia after their suppression in Bohemia in the twelfth century. The earliest records of a Jewish community in Trenčín date back to 1663 when a large number migrated from persecution in Moravia. Records are sparse. The first Trenčín rabbi was Israel Chaijim in 1791, who offered services in a wood synagogue, not far from its present location, but which burned down. After several reconstructions the community managed to build an imposing new synagogue in Moorish style that was opened in September 1913. The synagogue was taken over by the state in 1990 and converted into an exhibition hall, since there was no community any more to worship in it.

21. The Synagogue, about 1929

The Trenčín Jewish community was fully equipped to sustain its religious customs. They had a burial society, Chevra Kadischa, performing the ritual functions for the dead. There was a Jewish almshouse and a Jewish cemetery which is now the only Jewish institution remaining for burial of the last few members. The community operated a ritual bath (*mikva*), and supported a ritual butcher and slaughterhouse. There was a kosher meal service for the poor, a kosher hotel with a dinning room and a Jewish elementary school formed in 1800. In the 1930s, the school had 132 pupils. In addition, the community supported a thriving collection of voluntary organizations that in the 1930s increasingly concentrated on supporting Zionist movements, especially for the youth. Most prominent of these was Hashomer-Hatzair, which was also part of the international scouting movement.

The Jewish community consisted of about 2,000 souls out of a population of about 19,000. The Jewish population by the end of the 1930s thus accounted for about 10 percent of the town's inhabitants. It congregated in the large synagogue that even today is one of the largest public buildings in town. That is not remarkable since the Jewish merchants and legal or medical professionals provided much of the trade and services to perhaps as many as fifty surrounding villages.

The Jewish community raised its own taxes, in addition to all of the other state-mandated taxes, to support its own schools, charities, cemetery, ritual baths and the synagogue with a seating capacity of about one thousand. Women were placed on the balcony, which had separate entrances from the street while men prayed on the main floor. Small boys were permitted to visit their mothers on the balcony, but the little girls were discouraged from visiting their fathers on the ground floor. The wealthy merchants "owned" permanent seats in the temple for a substantial fee, charged depending on the location. Absence from services, especially on high holidays, was always subject to community disapproval. My family's pew was in a lesser location because Grandfather Philip did not believe that proximity to the lectern made any difference to God. My father's opinion was that the local rabbi was incompetent, which was an unforgivable condition that everyone recognized but only my father voiced in public.

It was a large Jewish community that was well integrated into the economic life. Community life was centered on the Jewish parochial school (the first five elementary grades) and the synagogue. There were many holidays that had to be kept. Adhering to the Jewish religion did not make much sense to the increasingly radicalized Zionist youth. The elders in the synagogue called for adherence to elaborate rituals that didn't make much sense to the young generation. What particularly grated on us was that all praying was done exclusively in Hebrew. I didn't understand it, with the minor exception for familiar phrases. The Jewish teachers did not teach the Hebrew language, although we had to memorize long passages which I suppose was good training for the brain cells. The irony in all that was that it was the anticlerical Zionists who insisted on teaching us modern Hebrew as a requirement for leaving for Palestine.

My father, although he was one of the leaders of the community (which was described as being a large contributor to charities) was known to be vocally critical of the local rabbi for never mastering Slovak so that most locals could understand him. So our community was in conflict, splitting the youth from the elders. On one hand, the presiding leaders demanded compliance with the traditional religious experience. On the other, there existed a simmering rebellion against the old rituals by those who had secular inclinations. Such sentiments were encouraged by the time I was about seven through my association with the local Zionist organization of Hashomer-Hatzair. This was a youth organization that was agnostic, socially conscious and fervently Zionist. They rejected the continuation of an existence in Slovakia and insisted on getting everybody to Palestine where free people would live in a communally utopian environment.

As conditions worsened, the Zionist influence became reinforced because their ideas offered anyone, who was not sufficiently wealthy to emigrate on their own initiative, a way to exit Slovakia. Hashomer members sang rousing songs that were emotionally uplifting. The singing in the synagogue, such as it was, would consist mostly of wailing. The Hashomer singing was militantly zippy and was enhanced with a large dose of marching music that was generously plagiarized from international sources. I loved to march down the main square loudly singing in Italian a song that made fun of Mussolini. Subsequently I found out that much of this singing was plagiarized from Russian socialists and vice versa.

Years later, I recognized that the leftist youth always had the best songs and the comeliest girls. That surely offered fewer distractions from ideologically more important matters. The songs and the accompanying dramatics as well as intensive outdoor activities, such as camping and hiking to exhaustion, offered unmatched comfort to the youthful rebels as the bad times were closing in on us starting in 1936.

Household Matters

Much of my childhood was occupied with chores of dragging wood from a deep basement with thirty-six very steep steps and then up to the first floor to the kitchen (twenty-two steps) or to the second floor laundry (another twenty-two steps). Twice a year my grandfather negotiated the purchase of a cartload of six-to-eight-foot-long tree trunks that were sold by the local woodcutters on designated market dates. The woodcutter then pulled into our yard and dumped the tree trunks so that another team of hired wood splitters could take over and chop the wood into small pieces that could fit our stoves.

The market days were specialized. Some were devoted to cattle trading, others to poultry and vegetables and others to clothing. Market days were always a colorful experience. They were events around which much of the community's commercial life revolved. I was also kept busy picking up blocks of ice from the local ice factory where the ice was made from the town's water supply. Most of the housewives in the community were buying much cheaper ice from local butchers who maintained icehouses where they kept river ice under a thick cover of sawdust which would be serving as protective insulation. The river ice had been hacked from the polluted river during the prior winter. The ice was available because the fast river passing through Trenčín froze solid just about every year. Keeping meat refrigerated with such ice was certainly not a sanitary solution. My mother offered that as a justification why strict dietary rules imposed by the Jewish community were a good reason why kosher was justified as guaranteeing a safe supply of all meat.

That made sense to me because one of the principal causes of chronic disease in Slovakia was stomach ulcer resulting from a combination of tainted food and too much alcohol. The water supply in the villages came mostly from local wells that could not be isolated from the effluents that seeped from the barns housing livestock and from the outhouses. Sewers would be available only inside major towns. The life expectancy was about fifty-five years, with the peasants' even less than that. Anyone over sixty-five was considered positively ancient and was probably an invalid. Women aged much faster than men. Women in their thirties were wrinkled. In their ubiquitous black clothing and a black headscarf they looked worn and unattractive.

The villagers were very poor but kept amazingly clean houses. Desperately impoverished widows occupied many of the hillside one-room log-cabin farmhouses. The high mortality rate and the emigration of many men produced that population. Invalid partizans would be picked up and cared for when wounded or when the severe winter weather made them immobile. Taking care of a partizan, especially when he or she was of a nonthreatening type, had the added advantage of filling the cramped space of a mountain cottage with an armed occupant at times when bands of soldiers, deserters, escaped prisoners of wars and even turncoat Nazi soldiers were passing through the mountain settlements seeking shelter and food. When my health failed late in January 1945, I was taken in by an old woman who for a few days fed me with milk, noodles and farm cheese until my partial recovery. That was an unselfish act of charity because the harboring of a partizan was punishable by execution. I had no money to offer, only fleas.

CUSTOMS

Kosher was carefully and meticulously followed. Together with my schoolmates I attended the obligatory morning services every Saturday. They were held in the largest classroom in the Jewish school, not in the large synagogue, which was reserved for more formal services.

The synagogue still is in existence today. It was built as a Neo-Romantic building in 1913. The building is of a central type with a central cupola, inspired by Byzantine architecture using a modern reinforced-concrete structure. Especially devoted religious elders used an adjoining small room for prayers as a tabernacle. It serves now as a memorial to local Jews murdered during the Holocaust. The huge central room under the cupola is now empty, following several unsuccessful attempts by the local government to convert it into a cultural center.

My grandfather Weiner saw to it that I attended without ever missing a service, because we all participated in it. These services were held in a school classroom and not in the more boring large synagogue. Children with good musical talent were chosen to sing the leading parts, usually adopting melodious versions of Eastern European liturgy or local variants of folk songs. In due course the soloists developed their own variations and it was always a source of great pleasure to expect a new musical embellishment demonstrated under the disapproving eyes of the elders who preferred more stylized and old-fashioned wailing.

The leading soprano and show-off was the daughter of a textile merchant in our neighborhood, Vera Suess, for whom I developed a lifetime crush since the age of five. My principal rival for the favors of Vera, such as sharing a chicken liver sandwich, is my lifetime friend Palo Ringwald (Ravid), now in kibbutz Dalia in Israel, whom I am still visit whenever possible. He reminds me that when he was eight he almost blinded me when he plunged a pen into my right eye as we quarreled over who would share lunch with Vera. The leading baritone was my lifetime friend, the al-ways-serious Franco Goldner, who now lives in Gothenburg, Sweden and with whom I still visit and talk by phone at least once a year.

I can still see the faces of various classmates, as refreshed by the obligatory annual class photograph. Very few survived the Holocaust. In 1995 the town of Trenčín honored me as a distinguished citizen. During the interview with the mayor I was asked what I thought of the town now. I told him that when I walk the streets I see ghosts everywhere. I would imagine images peeping out of windows and doorways when I walked the streets. These would be faces of the children with whom I grew up and still remember the way they were before the war.

22. The Faces I Remember to This Day, 1941

RELIGIOUS OBSERVANCE

We had a very intense religious life by today's standard, although I must say that there was an orthodox Jewish minority in Trenčín who con-sidered us improperly secular. We did not wear distinctive clothing and didn't display any outside markings of religious Jews, such as side locks or ritualistic underwear.

My only problem with being Jewish was the incomprehensibility of the liturgy, the archaic form of the prayers and the religious protocol that may have been applicable in former times under ghettolike existence. While I followed the required routines with meticulous care and was able to recite from memory long passages, I did not understand much of what I was reciting because I never managed to learn Hebrew, even while attending an exclusively Jewish school. For prayers to be acceptable, one only had to pronounce them in the proper form, with the proper intonations. Only later did I pick up a smattering of the Hebrew language. Even then the prayers did not make much sense, especially the unceasing pleadings. Later on I came to understand why I was to inherit the burdens of centuries of persecution and tears.

Sabbath was observed. The candles were lit on Friday night, and my mother blessed the challah bread (a pleated bread made of white flour, with butter and eggs). The Seders were a very important occasion and we did not shortcut the prescribed Haggadah (the liturgy for the occasion). We went through the whole ritual in detail while waiting for a truly sumptuous meal, which included drinking wine, the only time I was ever allowed to touch it. The wine was not particularly good, having been supplied by the rabbinical monopoly. To this day I still do not drink any wine, perhaps for that reason. It seems that our likes and dislikes get formed much earlier than parents suspect.

One of the most memorable events for me was the administration of an annual ritual by Grandfather Weiner. The day before Yom Kippur orthodox Jews perform *kapores*. It involves a ritual killing of a chicken to remind man what he deserves to receive for his sins against God, although my grandfather insisted (with disapproval from my father) that the real purpose was to ward off evil for the rest of my life. This involves swinging a screaming live cock three times over the head of the oldest male child. A prayer is recited and the animal is killed according to kosher law with a swift chop to the neck with an ax. Years later, when I had to dart across a road that was under machine-gun fire I had the ridiculous idea that I could not be hit because of *kapores*. I also discovered that anthropologists studying many tribal customs, including in voodoo incantations, a form of the cock slaughter ceremony, have witnessed a form of this ritual. It may just be perhaps a good idea for my three male grandchildren to benefit from such added life insurance, although I am sure that my American born wife would consider that an unacceptable form of primitive superstition.

Invariably, the religious experience is not the result of some theological discourse but a habit woven from the small patterns of family experiences during childhood. For instance, matzo balls in chicken soup to this day convey to me a memory of my mother's solemn pronouncement, repeated in exactly the same tone, with the identical timing, during the Passover feast, that this year the soup is *nicht schoen, aber gut,* meaning "not pretty, but good." Why this phrase has stuck with me to this day is something I cannot explain, but it still carries a magic memory imprint.

Religious injunctions were also subject for theological experimentation. One day, Franco Goldner and I were thoroughly bored with the daylong religious services during the mandatory fasting on Yom Kippur. As I recall it, it was on a Saturday when transgressions "earned" double demerits in the personal accounting ledger in Heaven that kept track of good deeds as well as sins. It was this double entry bookkeeping arrangement, which was my childhood version of religion, ethics and justice. Accordingly, if sins exceeded good deeds, your accounts would be transferred to Hell after you died. Franco and I figured that eating a small piece of pork sausage would be the most formidable way of testing the Laws. There was no thunder or lightning. Both of us felt badly about the entire incident, boisterously announced to our friends, but nevertheless still remembered when we met in Sweden forty years later.

LANGUAGE AND CULTURE

Until I entered school at the age of six, much of the conversation at home was in German, because that was the language in which my father conducted many of his commercial dealings with manufacturer's representatives who came to visit us from large commercial centers such as Bratislava, Brno, Prague and Vienna, to pick up factory orders. It was a reflection of the prevailing business relationships in those days that a traveling sales representative, picking up his semiannual order for merchandise, was also considered to be a source of commercial intelligence.

Salespeople were personal friends and were treated for lunch and sometimes for dinner at our table. These traveling salesmen were viewed as emissaries and were frequently more trusted as sources of information than newspapers. As salespeople, they were typically extroverts and exuberantly optimistic. I believe that these people were initially useful in encouraging my father to keep expanding business affairs. While peace prevailed, the salespeople kept delivering self-serving views about new and profitable business opportunities. Unfortunately, they also turned out to be an unreliable source of intelligence about the severity of the rising threats from Hitler. To this day I do not believe whatever any commission-earning salesman recommends.

With the solid record of my father's success based on rapid growth and on seizing opportunities, others overlooked I believe that it was my father's inclination to favor good news over bad news, that ultimately worked against us. That made him discount the rising risks until it was too late to do anything about them. My only evidence about this is the discoveries that my father started buying properties in 1935, at discount prices, from a number of Jews who were liquidating their assets. That's how my father, in partnership with Andor Kubiček, owner of the town's largest drugstore, ended up owning a large factory for making bricks and acquired well over a hundred acres of pasture and arable land.

Until I went to school, my family always employed governesses. These were widows, divorcees or otherwise unattached older ladies, mostly German-speaking non-Jewish women, who were passed on from one family to another until children did not require constant supervision anymore. My early experiences with the military date back to, I believe, the age of four, when my favorite governess, Ottie, always managed to arrange excursions, for "fresh air", to wherever the military companies were conducting training exercises. While the troops were ordered to allow me to watch how they were setting up their weapons, which to this day are my favorite toys, the officers were taking good care of Ottie. I cried when the fun-loving Ottie was summarily fired by my angry father for an infraction that I figured out years later to be something of a delicate nature. What was called "female matters" was a topic that was strictly prohibited from ever being discussed in front of me but nevertheless remained a source of unceasing curiosity.

FAMILY

My father was considered the patriarch of the family. Only after seeing the movie *The Godfather* did I understand some of the intricacies of our family relationships as well as his patronage of a large number of small retailers who depended on his financing of their merchandise inventories.

Father had three sisters. They married men who kept tiny food retail shops, although Schalk as well as Flack also had a license to sell liquor and beer. The closest relatives were Aunt Pavla Altmann in Trenčín (with one daughter, Alice), Aunt Erna Schalk in Košeca (with son Karol, daughter Elizabeth, and grandchild Ivan) and Aunt Irma Flack in Puchov (with son Josef). There were repeated visitations to and from the family for birthdays, anniversaries and when help was needed, which was often. I remember spending several summers with the aunts in the villages and getting to know my cousins, especially Karol who was studying engineering in Prague.

Much time would be filled up just keeping track who visited whom and how often. Most of the clan was economically dependent on my father. Family life was therefore intense and I do not recall any quarrels or scandals except when my mother's only brother, Bubbi (Eugen) Weiner, a revolver-carrying speculator from Prague, refused to pay back to my father a big loan.

There was no Social Security. The extended family depended on whoever was the wealthy member for support in hard times. Although I distinctly remember that my parents obtained passports and exit visas in 1938, the idea of leaving Trenčín and leaving the dependent relatives to fend for themselves was something that my father would not accept.

My mother always worked side-by-side with my father, keeping the same long hours. She was the cashier of the business. So my mother was a working mother, and that was very much the pattern in Jewish families. Grandfather Alexander also worked in the store in the morning, checking out outgoing merchandise as it was loaded on the trucks and then again in the evening, when the trucks came back with the inevitable returns that required giving customers credit.

After 1939, as the village stores of our relatives were closed down, some of our uncles came to live with us and worked wherever Father could find employment for them. However, as temporary residents, they were all swept by the first wave of deportations that started in the spring of 1942.

EDUCATION

In Trenčín, because of the large Jewish community, there was an exclusively Jewish school, which I described earlier. You would call it a parochial school because it was funded entirely by a Jewish community tax on the parents, based on the ability to pay, not on number of children. The school had three classrooms and a staff consisting of three teachers. The first classroom was for the first two grades and was taught by Mr. Brunner, who held that position for more than thirty years and was considered a trusted advisor to several generations of pupils.

The second classroom was for the third grade and taught by a slightly senile Mr. Santo ("no-see-no-hear Santo") who enforced a strict discipline by means of a bamboo rod hit hard across knuckles of an outstretched hand. I recall being a frequent target of Mr. Santo's hard-hitting attention, especially after being caught promoting birth control articles to my less daring, but snickering classmates, who found the entire performance a good break in their boredom.

The third classroom was for the fourth, fifth, and sixth grades. That is where the real education began, though the turnover among the teachers here was very high. I was lucky because my father managed to convince Josef Weiser to come and teach in Trenčín. Weiser was a refugee from east Slovakia, subsequently the editor of Pravda and Dean of the School of Journalism in the postcommunist regime until he was purged. I credit Weiser with my love for history as a way of understanding contemporary affairs. Weiser could hold the class spellbound for hours by making human history come across as an often-repeated tragedy.

To this day I remember the last week before the school was closed down early in 1942. Weiser described the destruction of Jerusalem by the Romans. The electricity for the school had been already cut off. Weiser started his highly descriptive and dramatic narrative on a dark wintry February afternoon. The class did not move and did not make a sound, although the room was ultimately plunged into complete darkness. I still visit Weiser whenever possible to cheer him up that at least one of his students still has a profound memory and respect for his teachings.

The school had a tiny room that was advertised as a "gymnasium." A local branch of the Makabi athletic association ran it, even though most of my experience in sports came from an ongoing game of a rough local version of rugby in which everyone above the age of ten and upwards could participate. Teams were usually chosen by lot, distributing little guys among the few big guys who ended up with most of the goals. Each goal was a space between two columns on the outer walls of the thirteenth-century fortress. Once in a while the older girls joined for an enjoyable game of body tackle. The schoolyard was covered with crushed stone. I believe that over several years it must have consumed, at least a square foot of my skin from knees and elbows.

However, the favorite occupation of my classmates was to conduct the game of cops and robbers in the cellars and bastions of the old crumbling fortress, which dominated the steep rocky hill on top of the valley. The cops wore a blue cloth ribbon on their right arm, the robbers a red ribbon on their left arm. Years later I found out that in the USA army war games the "blues" are always good and the "reds" bad. The game consisted of catching up with either a cop or robber and "killing them" by tearing off their ribbon. Considering that some of the chase took place on top of old crumbling walls that bordered deep pits, it still amazes me why nobody was ever maimed in the scuffles.

Anti-Semitism

As a child, almost all of my social contacts while I attended the Jewish school were exclusively with my classmates. From time to time, my father took me visiting the surrounding villages where his men had stores for distribution of Strassmann merchandise. I also got to know the families of my fathers chief assistants. I always had a great deal of exposure to people outside of the Jewish community, which was unusual. But, on an intense personal level, childhood relationships were largely a parochial, with my Jewish peers. That filled my social world, particularly during my early youth.

As a group, sporting youthlike gang behavior, we were quite active and tightly knit. Flowing through Trenčín is a river where we used to go to swim. Come to think of it, the river was actually an open sewer with dangerous rapids and sharp stones, although we did not think about it when we dipped in it because it was much more adventurous and free than the chlorinated public swimming pool from where we were excluded. At river bends there was an accumulation of muck through which we often waded. It was only after the war that I found out that even a neglected scratch could become a bad wound. Apparently some of the villagers bathing there died of tetanus.

Once in a while, other children threw stones at us and shouted, "Jew! Jew!" but we considered that as natural as mosquito bites. Until just before the deportations began in 1942 we did not have too many apprehensions about anti-Semitism because we recognized that we were different as well as isolated in a separate world. Only rarely was somebody mugged or beaten up. From about the age of seven I was a member of a militant Jewish youth group. We made sure that damage was minimized because we always went together as an organized pack.

Sometime in 1941 or early in 1942, when the school was disbanded, my father put me to work as an apprentice in a machine shop that repaired diesel engines that were used to drive threshing machines. In this way I followed the track of those who were preparing for emigration. My father also believed that any educated person should also possess nonintellectual skills on which to fall back in case of need. The crew in the machine shop consisted of rough characters, but they treated me well except for the local communist (a Spanish Civil War veteran) who resented me not because I was a Jew but because my father had been a prominent merchant. It is this experience that led me to the conclusion that anti-Semitism could also be as much a reflection of differences in economic class than anything that could be traced to religion. Although I tried to acquire "working class" credentials by volunteering to do jobs nobody else wanted to do, that did not wipe out the communist's dislike. As a matter of fact, when my nemesis became local deputy communist party chairman after the war he did not acknowledge my combat record even though he sat out the anti-Nazi uprising in prison from where escape was easy.

HASHOMER-HATZAIR

The group that I associated with was the local chapter of Hashomer-Hatzair because my sister Ella was already a member. They rented a little house in the slum district of Trenčín. We had meeting rooms there, but in the back there were also bedrooms for those who were preparing for emigration to Israel. An emissary from Israel, who was rotated from various posts, managed the building. I remember best Akiba Neufeld, now Akiba Nir, whom I visited in Israel twenty years ago and who occasionally corresponded with me when I became interested in the roles of Hashomer in the anti-Nazi uprising. He was a full-time professional who supervised the activities of the youth and devoted much time to those who were learning a trade. The purpose was to get young people prepared for life in collective settlements in Israel. Everyone who was learning a manual trade was apprenticed to small shops in Trenčín, particularly in carpentry, building trades and in repair of agricultural machinery.

Hashomer-Hatzair pursued a policy of aggressive Zionism. Hashomer leadership believed that it would require military action to create and then to defend the state of Israel. The purpose of such a state was to create a nonalienated Jewish community where anti-Semitism would not exist and the persecutions of the Jews in exile would disappear. Thus freed from oppression Jews could start building an existence that would enable them to cultivate a unique culture, without the heritage of always being identified by others as an "asocial" class. Much of this ideology was laced with utopian ideas about how to build an ideal state that would then allow the creation of ideal communities, where exploitation of the workers by owners of the means of production would not occur. I vaguely remember one of the major ideological underpinnings of Hashomer-Hatzair: the so-called Borochoff pyramid that attempted to explain why Jews were disliked and persecuted.

These concepts influenced me for much of my childhood and somehow shaped my early professional ambitions. The Russian philosopher Borochoff maintained that every nation should build its existence by relying on workers, artisans and peasants as the basis of state power (e.g. the base of the pyramid) and confine the intellectuals and business people only to a narrow "superstructure" of the state (the pinnacle of the pyramid). This view closely matched the writings of many utopians who believed that in a just state there would be no exploitation of man by man and where most of the citizens could be classified as "laboring classes."

These exposures have led me years later to devote much of my time to the study of the structure of organizations, only to discover that the Hashomer utopian assumptions were completely wrong. Societies that grew and prospered proceeded to evolve exactly in the opposite direction than had been visualized by the intellectuals. Those who were preaching about the dominance of the workers proceeded to capture power in favor of the administrators. I have spent the last twenty-five years doing research and authoring several books that show that the "information workers," who deal in intangibles, have taken over the "workers, farmers and operators" who deliver tangible results.

Only much later, when observing the youth revolts of the 1960s, did I come to realize that much of the Hashomer ideology was a blend of counterculture, fear, anticlerical atheism and backward-looking utopian dreams that could not visualize the rapid progression of society from its agricultural base to an industrial society and then to the current stage of development that can be characterized as "information-based economies." From the perspective of the events before the war, the agriculturally based communes to be built in Palestine of that period ignited a zeal that can be found only in religious movements. Only by understanding the psychology of the original Zionists can one comprehend the ideas that originally shaped the destiny of Israel. It was the utopian Zionists who had a disproportional influence on the organizations that engineered the creation of the Jewish state in 1948.

It is sad, and surely a personal tragedy for many, to hear now expressions of the deep disappointment with the failure to realize the communal vision of worker-based Zionism that originally characterized the sentiments of my many friends who chose to emigrate to Israel after the end of WWII. They dedicated their lives to pioneering something that was based on assumptions that would not fit the reality of the new circumstances when Israel became a country driven by the same reality of conflicting power struggles as can be found in all other advanced states.

The number of ten- to twenty-five-year-old youths in Trenčín could not have exceeded 100. Nevertheless, just about every ideological faction was represented here. Second to Hashomer (boys and girls just about equally balanced) was the religious Mizrachis, mostly boys, who shied away from sports and aggressive ideas. Then we had the Makabi group, devoted to physical culture in the tiny gymnasium. The Makabis had the sportiest girls who attracted attention from my more fun-loving schoolmates.

There was also a small Betar cell in Trenčín. All I remember of them is that they wore black jackboots, heavy black belts, and brown shirts and postured just like Nazi storm troopers. The gossip was that they were acquiring weapons from the advanced Czechoslovak arms industry and preparing for a takeover of Palestine by force. Whereas the lore of the Hashomer celebrated the Hagganah (the citizen militia defending the communal settlements against marauding Arabs) the ideology of Betar was portrayed by Hashomer leaders as dangerously fascist.

In this way the environment of our small provincial town offered, during my early youth, a good exposure to the views of social utopians, communists, and fascists as well as to variety of strongly held religious views. Those early formative years provided me with an inoculation against extremes that would be encountered in years to come.

FAMILY LIFE

Family life was concentrated in the little time that was available on weekends or religious holidays. My parents worked in the store starting very early in the morning, with a lunch break when the store closed down for an hour for my father's nap, and then continued until late in the evening or until the trucks making the rounds of the neighboring villages came back and all delivered merchandise could be accounted for. The store was open Saturdays as well as Sunday mornings whenever the public markets or fairs were open.

With little time available for vacations, this left time only for Sunday or holiday excursions either to the neighboring spas of Trenčíanske Teplice or Piešťany when we finally could afford our own passenger car.

I do not know why but most of my pictures from childhood were taken at swimming pools. Here is one taken approximately in 1937 at the Zelena Žaba (The Green Frog) Pool in Trenčianske Teplice. The older lady is Cecilia Kobler, Ilka Kubiček's and Fredi Kobler's mother, a prim and always self-righteous lady, who always tagged on fully dressed, including embroidered refinery. I believe it was the outing with Andor Kubiček. Next to my sister is my lifetime friend Peter Kubiček.

23. The Strassmann and Kubicek Family

Here and there we were taken to pose for formal photographs. I did not realize that many of the pictures would be taken for passports and visa applications. If there is one regret I have about my family relationships it is the total absence of communications about what was going on that could possibly affect us. Most likely, my parents believed that I could not be trusted, being an assertive and outspoken child. That distrust continued, to my great pain afterwards, to the very end in 1944.

There are very few family pictures available after conditions worsened sometime in 1942 and subsequent to eviction from our home. We had to give up our camera and could not afford the expense for developing photos.

Peril

My awareness about something going wrong starts as early as 1936 (at the age of seven) and was surely confirmed by 1937. A stream of refugees started coming from Germany. My father's house was always a way station for people who were collecting money for various causes. My mother was the chairman of WIZO, the Women's Zionist Organization, and on every public or private charity list. My father's partner in the brick factory venture, Andor Kubiček, was working with Jewish organizations abroad and was acknowledged as a point of contact for refugees. There was always a heavy traffic passing through our house because refugees could improve their chances of receiving support if they claimed that they needed money to bribe their way on the journey to Palestine.

Andor was a delegate from Slovakia to the Zionist congress in Basel in 1939. We knew what was happening in Germany not only from Zionist sources, but also from the steady stream of visits of German-Jewish sales representatives who had lost their jobs and were using their old contacts to obtain assistance. The prospects of what could happen to us was not discussed at the dinner table, or in any other manner, though I perceived rising anxiety. I was an outspoken child and there was always a worry that I would disclose something to the family or to employees that would upset my father's position as the anchor on whom everything depended.

I remember a particularly tearful incident where my father's best friend abandoned his wife because he wanted to leave Trenčín and she wanted to stay on account of close family ties. That incident happened one evening in our store after it was closed and I witnessed, unnoticed, the shouting and crying from behind one of the counters. Separation and divorce in families was then a totally unheard-of experience.

This beautiful woman, Sylvia, and her husband, Robert came to see my father to try to settle their differences. Robert wanted to leave instantly because he believed that Slovakia would be taken over by Hitler within a few weeks. He was a depressed person. He just wanted to go, leaving all possessions. It was not clear where he wanted to go. He just wanted to pick the family and leave, without further delays. Whether that was part of other marital problems or not I had no way of knowing, except that I observed subsequently, on frequent occasions, how family ties broke under duress when families were forced to make a choice of whether to abandon sure comforts for journeys to uncertain fortunes. I was happy that the mother and her daughter Ruthie stayed. Little Ruthie was by far the most beautiful girl in Trenčín. Both mother and daughter were killed after the first wave of deportations. Robert survived and raised a second family, in Australia.

Family relationships and behavior, largely dictated by convention and community traditions, fractured in families with flimsy relationships when a head of the family had to confront the wrenching decision of whether to flee, hide, rely on bribes for survival or just follow whatever authorities told you to do. Decisions were often shaped by the internal strength of families to act with resolution and to take advantage of whatever options were still available. Tragically, as time progressed, fewer and fewer options were left open and the inevitable death would not be open to further bargaining anymore. I think that one of the insufficiently explored studies about the behavior of families during the Holocaust concerns the enormous pain suffered, prior to starvation and the brutality in camps, when the conventional rules of family existence already ceased to apply.

That late-evening confrontation between Robert and Sylvia is something I remember as one of the early traumatic experiences to be repeated many times during the next seven years as husbands abandoned wives, mothers were separated from children and grandparents were sacrificed as a way of filling the prescribed quota for the next morning's deportation to what were euphemistically called "labor camps."

Although I did not know it at the time, from these observations emerged my instinctive understanding that one should never allow oneself to be placed in a position where there were no more choices left for what one could do. The central theme for my lifetime outlook was formed in the years when I defined personal freedom as an opportunity to choose from the maximum number of available opportunities for how and where to act.

EXPLORING ESCAPE

My father, who could follow news in English commercial newspapers, started preparing for emigration I believe as early as in 1937. I remember that because I was having ice cream and was told to quickly wash my face because someone wanted to take pictures for a passport and a photographer had just become available. For my father and our family to secretly take pictures for a passport would have been a compromising mistake in those days since others viewed us as exemplars of stability.

My father also started putting large-denomination bank notes away. Following age-old instincts of the Diaspora, he understood that when conditions would deteriorate sufficiently we could bribe our way out of the country. Whether that was a realistic possibility has bothered both my sister and me these days. Throughout the war, my father continued to be torn on what to do to save the family, between his parents who were still living and would never move, and the large number of relatives to whom he took it upon himself to maintain as an obligation to protect as long as he could. In each case, when a crisis arose, my father always chose loyalty to his parents and duty to his extended family before making the hard choice of saving those few who could be still saved.

Regarding the emergency fund there is an interesting story to be told that will give an insight into the relationship between my father and my mother. As my father was accumulating dollar and pounds sterling bills, he was giving all of the emergency funds to my mother for safekeeping because my mother was always the one who minded the family's financial affairs and acted as the cashier in the store. Such money could not be deposited in a bank and therefore my mother kept the money in a metal cigar box. To keep it well hidden from servants, my mother went up in the attic where the Passover dishes were kept and hid the box behind a steam radiator.

One day, I think it was early in 1939, and there was quite a bit of money accumulated, my father asked my mother to bring down the funds because Andor Kubiček was leaving for the Zionist Congress in Switzerland. Andor's objective was also to set up a Swiss bank account that would later finance our family's escape out of Hitler's reach. As an official congress delegate, Andor would then be able to obtain the necessary visas and travel tickets in Basel because any such attempt in Slovakia would become public. Keeping complete secrecy about our preparations for escape was essential because my father believed that perhaps the entire situation would somehow settle down. At the time of Andor's departure my father was not as yet ready to make a commitment to emigrate with all of the wealth and family ties remaining in Trenčín.

My mother went to the attic, opened the metal cigar box, and found that all of the paper bills got so badly charred that the dollar and the sterling bills fell apart on touch. When she had put the cigar box behind a radiator it did not fall all the way down into the space between the floor boards as intended but got jammed between the radiator fins. The metal box then acted as a heat amplifier. The only thing I remember — and I have told my children this story as a way of illustrating what marital bonds and family forgiveness is all about — is Father didn't say a word of reproach to my mother at that time and never again. In the later years the decision not to leave in 1939 was partially justified because of the sudden disappearance of the essential escape funds.

Kubiček went to Basel and started making arrangements for our family as well as for his wife Ilka, son Peter, and his mother-in-law. He did not succeed in Basel, and then tried again in Paris and then again in Lisbon, before finally departing for the USA, I believe sometime in 1942. My father, as a true partner, then took on the additional responsibility of taking care of and protecting the Kubiček family. Both Mrs. Kubiček and their son survived and emigrated to the USA in 1947.

Another member of the Kubiček family and a good friend of my father's, Fredi Kobler managed to leave Austria for France just in time to evade Hitler. In France he joined the combat corps being formed by exiled officers from the Czechoslovak army. As I understand it, Fredi, a magician when it came to adapting to changing conditions, successfully got aboard the last troop transport leaving from France for England just as the German army was rolling in to close all of the ports. The adversities of the war benefited Fredi. Taking advantage of undervalued real estate in London he started investing in hotels accumulating great wealth in very short order. Throughout my life, I learned to admire Fredi who possessed an instinctive capacity to know when to cut loose and when to invest whenever others were timid. Fredi enabled my escape from Czechoslovakia by registering me as a student in a school for wireless technicians in England. Subsequently he helped me during my first few years in the USA.

THE MINDSET

To understand what was going on during the years of the gradual tightening of Hitler's stranglehold on European Jewry, while escape was still possible to unlikely places such as Cuba, Argentina, Shanghai, Birobidjan (the Jewish state inside the Soviet Union), South Africa, Canada and even the land of most desirable haven for every refugee, the USA, one must enter into the mindset of Jews in Slovakia. Of course, Palestine was always on the top of everyone's list, but the idea of becoming an agricultural worker in a communal settlement, under steady fire from Arabs was not exactly appealing except to those who had started preparing for such an existence early in their youth.

The problem with the small-town Jews, those who were deported to annihilation camps first, was that they reflected a parochial view of the world. They had limited resources and an ingrained fear of any prospects that would require uprooting the family though emigration. At all times, the prospect of an efficiently executed genocide was totally alien and unimaginable. The conceptual model of how to deal with adversity was in the Bible. The exodus from Egypt, the Babylonian captivity, the reign of Greek despots, the destruction of the Jewish state by the Romans and the pogroms in Russia were historical events against which Hitler's threats would be judged. In each case the lesson of the Bible was that suffering only made the Jews stronger and more resilient. I must also say that the conservative influence of the local community leaders inhibited the making of a politically more realistic assessment of the Nazi threat.

As the lethality of the holocaust emerged only gradually most of the established leadership of the Jewish community continued to tranquilize the population in hoping that somehow they can make "deals" with their oppressors. This tendency to compromise and to minimize disruption in traditional lives finds its fullest manifestation in the deplorable role of the Jewish community leadership in administrative collaboration with the Nazis and with the local Nazi stooges in assisting in the mass deportations of Jews to annihilation factories.

There was nothing in the lessons communicated by the rabbis, nothing in the books of the Bible or in the Talmud to prepare the Jewish communities, consisting mostly of poor folks eking out a marginal living in the villages and small towns, to prepare them for the monstrous crimes that were being organized with the same German efficiency as their industrial prowess. Confronted with a gradually escalating terror, the tendency at every step was either to deny it, minimize it or, to choose procrastination as a preferred way of avoiding what had rapidly become evident as inevitable murder.

Culturally, the entire Jewish experience over centuries was always one of putting up with persecution, not resisting destruction and certainly never to taking up arms against occasional killings and persistent terror. One could always disperse, emigrate, negotiate, enter into bondage, bribe or simply relapse into poverty until the bad times passed. Fortunes were made, then destroyed and then rebuilt again somewhere else or by different means. Temporary or permanent conversions to Christianity or to the Muslim faith offered escape routes from losses of freedom, livelihood or accumulated wealth. Such culturally ingrained experiences of centuries of wandering from one country to another after expulsions, pogroms, lynching, mass murder or simple expropriation (which my father initially considered to be the worst-case scenario) always favored procrastination as the first and the most favored option.

That a large part of the Jewish community in Trenčín, who had the means to afford it, would pick themselves up in a biblical reenactment of the Exodus was never a practical solution. Except for a few who had connections in distant lands, most of the Jewish community did not have a feeling of urgency to flee when that was still feasible. There was this continual bargaining with a fate that could have perhaps been seen as inevitable if Jewish leadership would have taken a sober view of what was happening in Germany and which was a clear and well-documented intent to destroy European Jewry. This propensity to look for temporary "safe" assurances without the will to make hard decisions has been a theme that very much influences me throughout my life and my views that one should never accept or associate with anything that is evil. Out of that developed my lifetime instinctive reaction to run whenever there was anything fundamentally wrong with what I could not change.

The debates like "Well, it can't be that bad, well, maybe I'll do this, maybe I'll compromise on this, maybe it won't be that way, and, besides, I don't know what will be when I end up in a strange land," became a form of incremental rationalization that ended up in paralysis when all of the options for escape vanished. "Incremental rationalization," a term I believe to have formulated almost sixty years ago, has become one of the dominant themes for my understanding of what I have observed in the behavior of Holocaust victims. People, for a number of reasons, were forced to find justification for whatever position they took. All that self-delusion became a one-way itinerary toward destruction.

When escape was still possible was a question of timing, risk taking, cash and decisiveness. That varied from place to place, from family to family. Theoretically, one could start on a path of migrating to Palestine. It was a hard choice, but nevertheless a feasible one if one was committed to put up with hardships and lots of pain after leaving the comforts of Slovakia. The destinations out of Hitler's reach were numerous, as attested by stories from places as diverse as Palestine, Uruguay, Shanghai, Kenya, South Africa, and the diverse Caribbean islands, including Cuba. There was a Rumanian of dubious repute who came to offer us visas to Madagascar (it turned out to save a few). There were shady operators who were selling Jamaican visas for hard currency and then disappeared. The stories about betrayals of desperate refugees are now well documented. After all these risks are added up in terms of mortality statistics, in retrospect, those who at least tried to flee had a far better chance of succeeding.

Those who at least managed to get away incurred far lower risks than those who did not even try. My personal risk calculator continued to function even after my arrival in what is still the safest place in the world, the USA. I exercised it during the Cuban missile crisis when I removed my family to our summer cottage in Duchess County, in building a house in 1967 in a place surrounded by hills blocking a line of any nuclear burst from Manhattan, and by consistently selecting seats next to an emergency exit whenever I take an airplane trip. To this day I serve as the Emergency Preparedness merit badge counselor to the local scout troop and continue pleading for greater emergency funding as member of the local Emergency Preparedness Operations Center. I continue to be a well-armed supporter of the National Rifle Association. All my boys have been well trained in armed self-defense and two have qualified as sharpshooters.

Part III
Slovakia

The Noose

On the 1st of September, 1939, the date of the outbreak of WWII, our scout troop was camping in tents near Levoča, in the Tatra Mountains close to the Polish border. Early in the morning, the booming sounds of bombing came across the mountains north of us woke us up.

After raising the flag, Akiba Neufeld, our Trenčín leader, informed us that war had broken out. We had to vacate the camp instantly and go home. It was not clear whether the Germans would be occupying Slovakia immediately and taking anti-Jewish measures. The camp closed and we departed for home by train, singing on the way, welcoming war as a prospect for solving all our troubles.

On the first few days, life continued as before. My father's anxieties were visible. My usually calm mother was very perturbed. Nobody knew what would happen except that with the declaration of war by Britain, and France the following day, a number of jubilant optimists were spreading rumors that after a brief war the Germans would surely be defeated.

THE PATH TO WAR

After the abandonment of Czechoslovakia by the French and the British in the Munich peacekeeping agreement in September of 1938, the Germans occupied the Sudetenland. This was the borderland of what is now the Czech Republic. After vacating its border fortifications Czechoslovakia became defenseless from a military standpoint. By gaining a relatively small amount of territory as a diplomatic accommodation Hitler gained sufficient confidence to declare that he would destroy Czechoslovakia by occupying it later, which happened in March of 1939.

Starting in 1938, it was obvious that the Slovaks would be collaborating with the Germans to bring Czechoslovakia under the control of the German Reich. The dominant Slovak political parties announced full support of Hitler's expansionary plans. The nationalist and mostly Catholic Slovaks had been under Hungarian tutelage for centuries. They wished to make a deal with the Germans to form an independent Slovak state that would hitch its future to what looked like the winning side in the coming war. An independent Slovak state would also allow them to separate from the Czechs, a more cosmopolitan, Protestant, and formerly Austrian culture.

The separatist moves towards Slovak independence generated a glimmer of hope among the Jews that perhaps they would be treated differently than were the Czech Jews who would be subjected to severe restrictions as soon as they would come under German control. It was expected that Slovakia, as a German collaborator, would not be occupied by the German military and its population would not be subjected to the Nazi laws. It was assumed that Germany would not care much about controlling Slovakia because the Slovaks did not have an armaments industry like that which the Wehrmacht coveted in the Czech lands. Such speculations added to rationalizations that doing nothing and waiting for possibly favorable outcomes would be the most prudent position for Slovak Jews to take.

Indeed, the Germans did not occupy Slovakia because they were concentrating on getting ready to wage war on France and England. Meanwhile, everything continued without much disruption. Only the most agile Jews left without delay to whatever country would accept them. The exodus to Palestine was also speeded up but that was seen as mostly applicable to young Zionists who had been training for hardships and for physical labor. Most of the Jews who lived in Slovakia were merchants, petty business owners, professionals, and tradespeople who were used to a relatively good level of comfort. There also were elderly people, families with small children, and owners of property who just couldn't visualize picking themselves up and going where they would have to start from the bottom rung of the economic scale, in lands where speaking in a foreign language would be obligatory.

The Jews who left first were wealthy lawyers. I remember two families who had cultivated connections with families abroad. One was the family of a Trenčín lawyer named Ringwald who successfully unloaded his large real estate holdings as early as 1936 at huge discounts. When the Slovak state was formed, Ringwald was already settled comfortably in England. The other family was the Petscheks from Prague who were prominent bankers with well-established international connections. Their children had been educated in fine English schools. When the invasion from Hitler's armies became imminent they picked themselves up and transferred to their residences elsewhere. Families that had established links with relatives abroad, a centuries-old survival practice by Jews, and had deposited money in safe banks found it relatively easy to get a visa and to leave without much discomfort.

Meanwhile, my father's business affairs did not change. As a safeguard my father tried to arrange it so that a trusted associate could take over the business in case it would be threatened with confiscation. The worst-case scenario among the remaining Jews was to anticipate loss of property. Effort was therefore concentrated on ways for assets to become expropriated by people with whom they had a trusted relationship.

With only few options left regarding of who would become eligible to take over, my father started strengthening his relationships with a prominent member of the Slovak right wing, a leader of the local Hlinka Party who was also associated with the Catholic church. Mr. Bonko was a small shopkeeper who had a good relationship with my father, which had developed over many years as a retail distributor of merchandise from our wholesale firm. Bonko also had an ambitious wife who was eagerly looking towards acquiring possession of Strassmann properties.

Father's anticipations were correct. The expropriations (aryanization) took place at the end of 1939. The name Strassmann came down from the marquee on top of our store and the name Bonko & Strassmann went up. Mrs. Bonko took over the cash register. My father became a poorly paid bookkeeper whose experience was essential to keep the enterprise operating. That arrangement lasted for only a short time. Meanwhile we had to vacate our living quarters facing the street so that the Bonko family could move in. Shortly thereafter Bonko took over the entire firm under the name of Jan Bonko. His family now occupied the entire house my father built in 1934.

The Legal Phase

The decisive step in shaping the future of Slovak Jews was the proclamation of the Slovak independent state in March of 1939. Jozef Tiso, a Catholic priest, became prime minister. The Hlinka People's party became the only party allowed to function legally. Slovakia became an ally of Germany and provided rail and road access for the Germans troop movements. After the German attack on Poland and later on Russia, Slovakia was also to provide fighting troops. In October 1939 Tiso was elected president; pro-Nazi Voytech Tuka became prime minister; and the rabid antisemite, Šano Mach, head of the Hlinka Guard, became the minister of the interior. This team set out to organize the machinery for the subjugation and in due course the destruction of the Jews.

To gain legitimacy in expanding Hitler empire the Slovaks pledged that their new state would adopt the Nuremberg laws that would escalate the restrictions placed on Jewish life. In April 1939 the new Slovak state enacted anti-Jewish legislation, by an overwhelming parliamentary majority, defining the status of Jews along religious rather than racial lines. This distinction was a departure from the usual Nazi approach that had been followed in every other European country that came under German control. This reflected the fact that Slovakia was a Catholic country, ruled by a priest who saw all distinctions among people in theological terms. I believe that this difference influenced subsequent events when the deportations of Jews to annihilation camps were suddenly stopped in the fall of 1942 by what is now claimed to be interventions, yet unproven, from higher quarters of the clerical hierarchy.

In many respects, the Slovak approach to the resolution of what came to be called "the Jewish question" was seen initially as less damaging than the practices followed by the Nazis in other lands. Consequently Jews rationalized their circumstances by accepting that they would have to bend to the laws. They accepted that the only way to survive was to comply with Slovak regulations as long as this would clearly define, in an orderly manner, what is not permitted. The Slovaks obliged and created an elaborate set of rules and restrictions that the existing bureaucracy could administer as an extension of customary administrative processes.

In August 1940 SS *Haupsturmfuhrer* Dieter Wisliceny, Eichmann's representative from the Reich Security Main Office, arrived in Bratislava as an adviser on Jewish affairs. The Hlinka Guard and the *Freiwillige Schutz-staffel* (Slovak volunteers in the SS) were then reorganized on the model of the SS. They were given the responsibility for implementing anti-Jewish measures so that the existing administrative bureaucracy would carry out the persecution exactly as was dictated. The sequential order of how such measures would be implemented was dictated by a calculated progression of how to strip the Jews of all their property. This was set up so that this would require a minimum of effort, while rewarding the loyal backers of the new regime with ill-gotten wealth, without creating internal dissent.

On September 9, 1941, the Slovak government promulgated an elaborate body of anti-Jewish legislation and regulations. It contained 270 articles, such as requiring Jews to wear the identifying yellow Star of David, making them subject to forced labor without pay and evicting them from specified towns, locations as well as from specifically designated streets and houses (listed by house numbers).

For as long as it was the Slovaks implementing Nazi rules one could always hope to be dealing with people one had always done business with. Under such circumstances the age-tested patterns of Jewish survival, through negotiating for some sort of accommodation, could be tried again. That did not work. The machinery that still reflected habits remaining from the days of the Austro-Hungarian empire that had been gone for only twenty years would proceed to grind the Jews into submission.

THE STRANGLEHOLD

The first restrictions came late in 1939. This is evidenced by the dates in a collection of documents I donated many years later to the Holocaust Museum in Washington, D.C. The papers reveal the bureaucratic thoroughness by which laws and regulations were deployed for the progressive degradation of Jewish lives. In this case we have a collection of over fifty certificates and receipts that document the sequence in the destruction of the life of a Jewish innkeeper from a village nearby.

The dates on these documents, salvaged from a shoe box by a friend of my sister, demonstrated the successive steps in how the Slovak state, imitating the proven German's proven thoroughness — except not as brutally — used perfectly legal procedures for the economic strangulation of Jews. In each instance this was accomplished by passing a law that was always approved by the unanimous vote of representatives elected by popular vote.

The innkeeper was a WWI invalid who had received in the early 1920s a coveted liquor license as a privilege that was granted to wounded veterans. In the shoebox was a rumpled copy of an elaborate legal measure stating that Jews cannot qualify as innkeepers. Within sixty days everybody who had been a Jewish innkeeper would have to give up his license and hand it over to a designated local supporter of the Slovak state. The only qualification for the new innkeeper would be an endorsement from the local Hlinka Guards, the self-appointed paramilitary guardians of the state.

It is noteworthy that many of the postwar claims by Jews for restitution of property were rejected on the grounds that such expropriations were legally valid because they were based on laws passed by parliamentary due process of a sovereign state. Accordingly, there were no crimes committed against the Jews.

I must add that the custom of legal expropriations has a long history in much of Eastern Europe where frequent changes in the regimes always ended up having an existing property holder replaced by whoever was the latest political favorite. Violent changes in government were also accompanied by local uprisings to evict holders of old privileges while wholesale looting was taking place. To much of the Slovak population the evictions of the Jews offered a legitimate way for acquiring assets with a minimum of effort.

Taking property from whoever lost protection of the state has been endemic to that part of the world and was continued by the communist government with a zeal that exceeded even that of the Nazis. It must be difficult to the younger readers of these pages, especially if they are Americans, to comprehend the circumstances I found after the end of the war. Wherever I walked in my hometown, while still in Slovakia, I could see evidence of theft.

LEGALIZATION OF THEFT

After you remove the livelihood of all Jewish innkeepers the question still remained: What to do with them? Two of my uncles were innkeepers making a very modest living and who now became instantly destitute. Next, as the war continued with unabated German victories, the Nazi methods called for the isolation of the Jews from the rest of the population. The Slovaks would then pass another regulation that Jews could not have radios that had shortwave frequency capability. Shortly thereafter, all radios were prohibited. Then, you could not have a telephone or a vacuum cleaner or a camera.

For instance, if you had a radio, or any item on the prohibited list, you had to hand it over to the local police who then issued you a well-crafted formal receipt. The police then proceeded to distribute the radios to the Hlinka party faithful who were now charged with the added responsibility to house-check how well the Jews were complying with the rising number of restrictions. Although this process was aimed at increasing the subjugation of Jews, it also served as a means for the party loyalists to impose control over an orderly distribution of loot to only selected recipients as well as to drag more citizens into becoming eager participants in state-sanctioned robbery.

After the spring of 1940 the sequential collection of the receipts in the shoebox increases. The burden is now placed on every Jew to show compliance with restrictions and to be able to prove that nothing remained hidden. The steady stream of restrictive laws and administrative regulations now becomes enshrined in a detailed set of codes. Any violation could then be used as pretext for imposing additional penalties. For example, the state decreed, in a detailed proclamation appearing in the daily press, what clothing was prohibited and what apartment would have to be given up. Those seeking to take possession of choice living quarters assisted in the compilation of such lists. In a number of cases, additional locations were added as a special favor. In effect, that evicted the Jews from their quarters on short notice. If you lived in a house above a store on a street where business was conducted you had to hand over the keys to a preselected party functionary. The evicted family had to then seek whatever housing they could get, and that was usually in much smaller and poorer quarters. The furniture would remain, by default, with the new occupants of their original homes. For instance, our partially disabled innkeeper now ends up in the back of a farmer's barn with only the barest essentials.

The collection of documents from the now destitute innkeeper keeps growing rapidly. It shows receipts for cameras (authorized by a separate law), fur coats (another law), jackets with fur collars (a regulation), valuables such as jewelry, certificates of declaration about bank accounts owned, proof that there were no debts payable to anyone, a receipt for the payment of "transportation costs" for the only son now departing to a work camp in Poland, and finally a notice to report in the morning to the local railroad station for "transfer to an unspecified location." This required prepayment of a "transportation fee" of 500 Reichmarks each for the innkeeper and his wife. That was a huge amount in those days. The nominal worth of one Reichmark was about US $0.45 in 1940. In today's prices 500 Reichmarks would be equivalent to about $2,250, in current prices based on the tenfold depreciation of US currency since 1940.

All of the officially stamped receipts for property and persons were recorded on mimeographed forms. These were usually headed by the phrase "According to Paragraph xx the undersigned acknowledges receipt for yyyy." All of this was done to preserve orderly thievery and to keep up appearances that a perfectly legal business transaction was taking place.

JEWS AS PROPERTY

Unbeknown to the purchaser of the cattle-car fare to Poland was the arrangement by the Slovak state to turn over this money to Eichmann's SS for setting up and operating annihilation camps. Slovak law defined such transfers as exchanges of property, absolving the Slovaks of further responsibility for their citizens. With the state depriving the Jews of all civil rights, Jews could be now treated legally as property, thus invoking ancient Roman doctrine that governed the conduct of slave trade.

Slovakia was the only country in Europe that paid, in hard cash out of state funds, the Germans for the deportations of Jews. By making this a property transaction in which the legal title for human beings was transferred to another sovereign state, the Slovaks government believed it would be absolved of any blame for whatever the Nazis would do with the Jews. I still remember how the Slovak press featured numerous stories showing pictures of well-fed Slovak Jews sewing German uniforms and contributing to Nazi victory while working in presentable factories. Such stories were used to tranquilize whatever conscience may have lingered within the population. Propaganda was used to assure the remaining Jews that survival would be possible until the war was over.

After the war, the shipping registers listing the names and the money paid by the Slovaks to the SS for the dispatching of Jews to Poland remained the principal documentary evidence about transporting families to certain death. The existence of such lists may have started to haunt a few Slovaks, and especially the catholic clergy.

After over 80% of the Jewish population was disposed of to annihilation camps in Poland, by the end of the summer of 1942, someone in the hierarchy must have become apprehensive. Thought had to be given to possible consequences, in case of the then unlikely prospects, that the Germans could lose the war. I am convinced now that such realization could have coincided with the news that started percolating that the German war progress on the eastern front was not proceeding well. Any doubts about an eventual German victory must have contributed to such unease.

Family Deprivations

The next shock administered to our family took place early in 1941. We were ordered to move from the two back rooms of our well-appointed six-room residence to a small two room apartment near the Lutheran church. There was a small kitchen and one wood-burning stove to heat it. Father could arrange such a move because he found out that the street number on that address was somehow omitted from the prohibited list.

Vacating the family house we had owned was an eviction and expropriation, not a sale. Most of the architect-designed and built-in furniture was left in place for the Bonkos to use.

Ella and I slept in the living room. Our parents occupied the bedroom that also doubled as the storage room and pantry. I recall that Mother kept on top of the cabinet fruit she occasionally received from childhood school-friends. It was my job to inspect individual pears to see which ones would be turning brown so that they could then be eaten. Considering the circumstances, the living conditions in the new place were not bad. Father arranged for the move to be done as smoothly as possible.

I think the whole thing was tolerable because nobody could have guessed what would be the outcome of the war and what fate was awaiting us. The general sentiment in those days was in the form of repeated monologues: "The war is here, but the war will come to pass, and somehow we'll survive"; "Jews have survived adversity before"; "There have been situations before when bad times have come and gone"; "How bad can it get?" and "Surely nobody would wish to kill us."

The borders had been closed since mid-1939. Jews could not get passports. One could leave only illegally, assuming that there was a visa issued to a country that would accept a Jew. At this point, it was impossible for our family to contemplate escaping illegally. To move would require also transporting also a retinue of grandparents, dependent relatives and children. The great majority of Jews were now stuck in Slovakia physically as well as psychologically. The only choice that was left was in how to learn to submit to the new regime while suffering the least amount of hurt. That meant applying the lessons learned by Jews in how to survive over centuries while surrounded by never-ending hostility.

The only glimmers from the rapidly closing outside world were occasional messages smuggled in by the most devious ways imaginable. I vaguely recall an aborted effort to escape from the Nazi grip by moving our friend Fredi Kobler's mother to San Remo near Genoa in Italy sometime in 1940. It appears that because of treaties dating back to the fourteenth century San Remo was a principality retaining some of its ancient rights to act as a sovereign state. Fredi's mother actually left Slovakia but ultimately returned for reasons I cannot recall. I only mention this incident as an indication that the Nazi net had holes, which could be exploited if audacity and money were present. A few of the more venturesome actually managed to get out via Rumania and then through Turkey to Palestine.

It is hard for me to explain now, sixty-two years later, what my feelings and reactions were to the rapidly changing surroundings. I could only sense the growing anxiety of my parents and an increased sense of isolation from the community. My parents did their best to protect us, largely by keeping quiet about their own troubles and resorting to speaking in Hungarian whenever confidences had to be exchanged. I was never told about any of the actions or contingencies that my parents were planning for. Little was disclosed to us as children, in the fear that we would disclose damaging information or inadvertently blab about it.

PLUNDER

From the snippets of conversation between my parents I could gather that our property was gradually disposed of as gifts for favors. We had beautiful Persian rugs. The discussion was whether to leave the rugs for the Bonkos without offending them or to make better use of this asset as graft in return for some administrative concessions from corruptible officials. I also remember the debate about what to do with our expensive Contax camera, which was given ultimately given away as appreciation for some unspecified accommodation. We started shedding things voluntarily because they were going to be taken away anyway, so we now might as well get a small advantage from each transaction.

After the Liberation, many of such objects remained in the hands of people who claimed these objects were legitimate gifts received in return for favors. That poisoned my sentiments about remaining in Slovakia as an inhabitant. With the coming threat of a communist takeover I anticipated a repeat performance of the long history of plundering and repression whenever a political upheaval took place.

Much of the accumulated wealth in Slovakia even today can be traced to expropriations of Hungarian landowners after the end of WWI, to expropriations of the Czechs in 1939, to expropriations of the Jews in 1940-1942, to the expropriations of Germans in 1945, to expropriations of the capitalists in 1948 and to the large-scale pilfering of State property (now owning it all) after the demise of the communist regime in 1998. The history of politically-sanctioned injustice in Slovakia has a long pedigree. It has made a lasting political imprint on the civil behavior of inhabitants in that part of the world. Habits that favor oppression, plunder, theft and corruption will not be expunged for generations to come.

The conduct of the population has been influenced by their cynical understanding that it was advantageous to support the legitimacy of looting by means of a legal framework that would protect the rights as thieves. That is why, from 1939 through 1941, my father was burdened with a flood of declarations and affidavits to account for all of his property and all of his financial relationships. What was different in 1941 and in 1942 was the Nazis' intent to first relieve all Jews of their civil liberties, then property and finally culminate even existence by deprivation of their lives.

When state-organized plunder takes place, there are incentives for the government to co-opt party faithful to acquire a stake in thefts. That will assure loyalty, create a cadre of dedicated henchmen, and add to state coffers without added costs of taxation. When the Slovaks decided that Jews may not reside on this or that street or not own such and such possessions the regulations were drafted, with the participation of local operatives, who were already settling among themselves who would take ownership of which property. That's why the Jewish experience in Slovakia was never characterized by brutal nighttime roundups of an entire community, as happened elsewhere in Eastern Europe, but by the deliberate process of planned impoverishment so that nothing would escape the distributions that were managed by the local Hlinka Guard merchants. One could also describe the gradual destruction of the Jewish community as a cleverly conceived and self-financing business venture.

This phase took place from June of 1939 and lasted until March of 1942. When the Jews were finally ground down to abject poverty and despondency, they were now set for shipment to annihilation camps over a period of several months, one trainload at a time. This process had every appearance of involuntary yet orderly eviction of unwanted tenants rather than corralling a herd headed for slaughter.

The Slovaks merely reenacted their frequent experiences in which any regime changes would always make available spoils for distribution to the supporters of the new regime. Previously that had occurred in Slovakia during revolutionary changes, regardless of ideology or religion. For a while the Jews were fooled into believing that what was happening now was merely a more extreme replay of an age-old phenomenon that was survivable.

What made the Jewish holocaust in Slovakia historically unprecedented was its scope. Perhaps as much as 15 percent of all real property in Slovakia had been confiscated. The Slovak holocaust was also more lethal, with 93 percent of the Jewish population ultimately murdered. What was also different from all of the other prior expropriations was the well-organized persistence that was guided by a legal bureaucratic process that was set up to disguise the Nazi ideology. Years later I summarized this era as a step-wise process for bureaucratic organization of preplanned murder.

BUREAUCRATIZATION OF GENOCIDE

What imprints into my memories about the happenings between 1939 and 1942 are the meticulous administrative procedures that were inexorably progressing toward the "final solution," which would take place in the form of institutionalized genocide. The unique Nazi form of genocide, as opposed to the mass-killings of the Armenians, American Indians, Tutsi tribesmen, Kosovars, or Cambodians, was driven by a well-conceived, systematized process optimized to execute racist laws efficiently. Although well over a hundred million people have been killed in genocidal acts since the end of WWII, only the German form, with the exception of Stalin's executions, could be categorized as industrialized management of civilian death. The leaders were not homicidally deranged executioners but well-trained and university-educated death engineers.

The Slovak version of genocide imitated the German model in that it took special pains to make sure that all actions taken against the Jews were procedurally correct. A number of Western states have recognized the acts passed by the Slovak fascist government as laws that were passed by a duly elected legislature, following a well-documented judicial process.

The system was rigged to eliminate the possibility of any appeals. Consequently, the Slovak genocide was only rarely accompanied by overt acts of personal violence such as was customary whenever SS troops took over, such as was the case in Poland and newly occupied Soviet lands. In Slovakia the Jews meekly marched toward their destruction in an orderly form that was organized and administered by their own community leaders.

The Machinery of Genocide

These experiences have now sharpened my full comprehension of how the machinery of a totalitarian state can be applied to destroy any population it chooses to persecute. It shaped most of my outlook on politics and on what forms a civilized society must take and nourish to safeguard the rights of individuals. My views of the dynamics of the Holocaust differ from much of the accepted lore. Large shares of the published Holocaust stories describe brutal beatings, shooting, murder, suffering, and starvation. Those are all true and horrible. But I find that insufficient attention has been devoted to documentation of what had preceded those atrocities. The German forms of the orderly industrialization of death are historically unique. The organization of the machinery of the Nazi-supported police states in France, Belgium, Holland, Hungary, Austria, Greece, Croatia, and Italy into agents of executions of the Jews offers case studies on how easy it is for a dominant military power to wipe out commitments to law and justice that these countries boast in their Constitutions.

Young people nowadays may have difficulty in getting into the mindset of the Nazis from the endless description of horror and suffering that characterizes much of the Holocaust literature. It is important for the new generation, reared in freedom and luxury, to gain an understanding of how every modern state, and particularly a police state that acquires the computerized capacity to monitor everybody's action, has the capacity to pervert its institutions to become instruments of organized genocide or slavery very efficiently.

The idea that government could leverage information technologies for complete control of its population became a popular topic in 1984 on account of George Orwell's book with that title. Orwell described the operations of a society run by a dictator who used ubiquitous television cameras to spy on everyone, at all times. From a technical standpoint I found a visually monitored police state economically and operationally unfeasible. For instance, I calculated the percentage of the population that would have to be employed to keep track of every corner of every room as well as of every vehicle at all times, without errors. The cost of setting up an auditing system to assure perfect compliance as well as the expense for videotaping everything would be economically crippling. Indexing, storage and context-based retrieval of such a huge volume of videotaped evidence cannot be performed, even with today's advanced technologies.

It just happened that while I was speculating about Orwell an international group of independent scholars decided to convene in 1983 a three-day meeting in Geneva to explore "Orwellian Threats" to society. Harlan Cleveland, the former US under-secretary of State and a great humanist, headed this group. I delivered a paper that offered, in sufficient technical detail, how a police state could use computerized networks for control over media, education, consumer spending, who ate what, as on all personal movements. By that time I had already witnessed at Xerox the potential of Arpanet networks to deliver a well-functioning Orwell-type society at a low cost. The Geneva meeting took place before the growth of the Internet, Google, and RFID (radio frequency identification) tags. The meeting participants, many of them from underdeveloped countries, did not find my scary scenario plausible and certainly not manageable by existing political institutions. One of these days, I will publish my Geneva paper and show how we are making "progress" to acquire technological capabilities that are potentially more dangerous to the freedoms of a civil society than weapons.

EVERYDAY LIFE

The Jewish school was closed sometime in 1940 or early in 1941. To keep me educated as well as occupied my father saw to it that I had private tutors. The quality of my education greatly improved. There were teachers who were friends of my father and were ready to help out. I particularly remember a demanding professor of mathematics and physics, Prof. Vikar, from the local gymnasium, which was a combination of high school and junior college. Vikar made me an assistant to keep the physics instruments in his laboratory in working condition. Prof. Kumprecht taught chemistry and geography. These professors did not earn much money and so they were always looking for tutoring jobs even for the pennies my father could offer. I also started learning English with Lucy Muller, a refugee from Austria, and continued my piano lessons with Mrs. Dubnicay, the hypersensitive wife of a district criminal judge. How my father and mother could afford all of such expenses still escapes my comprehension since Father's income was minimal and my mother was unemployed. I guess that teaching the son of a leading local citizen was viewed more as an act of charity than business.

During the tutoring years, I acquired studying habits that served me well in years to come. In the Jewish school the children were crowded into three classes covering ages from six to fifteen. In 1942, my class had an age range from nine to fifteen. It also included children with all sorts of disabilities. Time was wasted and the lessons were utterly boring because we all had to sit still and listen to uninteresting lectures that catered also to slow learners. There were very few textbooks and most of the tutorial material was gained from what was written on the blackboard with chalk.

Under the tutoring arrangement, because time was limited, the lessons were well organized for maximum progress. I had to study harder and with greater attention than ever before. These conditions forced me to acquire a life-long habit to rely largely on independent learning from books instead of listening to lectures.

THE YELLOW STAR

I started wearing the yellow star early in 1942. Instituting the distinct identification of all Jews, with the associated registry of every soul, would then become a precursor for the deportations to Poland. The Hlinka Guards wanted to make sure that they could nab everybody at will to enforce the yellow star rules and to make it easy to round up people on a deportation list.

There was a limited supply of yellow stars because they had to be firmly sewn onto individual garments. The stars were made in Jewish workshops and were distributed through the local Jewish community. How and where to place the yellow star was a topic of much discussion even though the regulations were explicit. Which jacket do you put it on if you had more than one jacket? How do you place it if you have a wide collar that would partially cover the star? My paternal grandmother was of a very small stature. She would not accept the yellow mark of indignity. Somehow she found a large pocket book that could be carried in an unassuming manner so that it completely covered up her identity markings. She was a very old lady and nobody ever bothered her, although she hardly ever went out of her tiny room after the wearing of the star was enforced more zealously.

Wearing the yellow star in a small town, where most people knew one other, became an unceasing source of embarrassment. That was precisely the effect that the Hlinka Guard intended to create as the ultimate public humiliation while the progressive stripping of one's dignity was taking place over a three-year period. Having no radio, no books, no movies, no music, no furs, no privileges to attend any entertainment or restaurants while being limited to only prescribed places, and only during appointed times, were degradations that could be borne as private deprivations. Wearing a yellow star was a public and dehumanizing disgrace. It invited mugging from a few hooligans who enjoyed harassing Jews, who were now totally inhibited from ever hitting back.

Deportations

The first deportations began in March of 1942. The deportation lists were compiled by the local *Judensraat* (Jewish Community Council) based on a quota received in advance. The deportation list was then handed over to the local Hlinka Guard command supervised by a German crew of only two or three Gestapo officers who were mostly Slovaks of German origin. The entire process was driven by schedules when a freight train would arrive at a siding in the freight yard of the local passenger railroad station and be ready to be loaded to full capacity. The deportation quota set for the Trenčín district was calculated depending on the carrying capacity of the freight cars and the number of cars available. For maximum efficiency this called often for jamming as many as eighty persons per car.

The Jewish Council was handed a demand for Jews meeting specified requirements. As I recall, young men were deported first under the guise of needing labor to support German military needs, though I am convinced that the real purpose was to get rid of all potential sources of resistance. Next came young women deported for the ostensible purpose of sewing winter uniforms for the troops on the Eastern front.

The entire operation was organized for efficiency. Only a handful of Germans were needed to hand over orders to the local black shirts who in turn passed the quota on to the *Judensraat* with copies to the local police and sometimes also to the local gendarmes, if the local police could be bribed for premature disclosure of what would happen. The police were municipal and largely under the control of the local government. As career civil servants they were relatively well integrated into the community. They could bend some of the rules for Jews they knew personally. The gendarmes were the enforcement arms of the state and were better armed because their primary purpose was to maintain civil order, especially if there was any threat of riots. They were bureaucratically compliant to orders from the central government and did what they were ordered to do.

For the roundups and for the supervision of the loading into the freight cars the local policemen did most of the work to reflect favorably on the legality of the deportations. The Hlinka Guard usually remained visible to make sure that nothing improper happened and to apply force when that was necessary, which did not happen in the customarily orderly Trenčín. Whatever brutality was applied it was by the lower ranks of the Guard. These men were usually uneducated opportunists leveraging the fascist regime as a means for upgrading their social and economic status. The primary objective of these people was to make sure that the property of the Jews was immediately sequestered and properly recorded. This was the means by which the Hlinka Party acquired wealth for distribution to its supporters.

At the entrance to the main square of Trenčín a former Jewish clothing store was converted into a pawnshop where items that had been removed from abandoned Jewish homes were laid out on tables to be picked over, for negligible prices, on the days immediately following a deportation. Although all of the more valuable items were long gone, peasants from neighboring villages attending the usual Sunday market day after church services used the proceeds from the sale of farm products to load their carts with Jewish goods. This store was besieged after the morning mass. Those who came late were usually delayed by their Confession.

Poor Jews were likely to be deported before rich Jews as a way of gaining more time to shake out from desperate families whatever valuables were still hidden. Jews in villages were deported prior to Jews from the city so that the distribution of property to local Guard functionaries could take place to secure the loyalties of the countryside population. With no more Jews remaining in the villages the opportunities for finding rural hiding places were largely cut off, while the few remaining Jews moved into towns where organized deportations were easier to set up.

What would be subsequently labeled as systematic "ethnic cleansing" was actually perfected in Slovakia as a well-planned systematic sequence. This was accomplished with the least amount of violence and at hardly any cost, while delivering instant benefits to a large share of the population. The point I am making here is that the annihilation of the Slovak Jews was proceeding with a concerted effort to disguise its criminality while leveraging it for maximum political advantage to the fascist regime. The progressive character of these crimes helped initially to tranquilize both the Jews as well as the Slovak population from comprehending the enormity of the unfolding crimes.

The organization of the deportations was aided by meticulously recorded census data showing age, occupation, religion as well as real estate assets. This demographic data was further refined after 1940 by elaborate surveys of Jews to include information such as savings accounts, currency holdings, insurance policies, and itemization of all valuables (including carpets, fur coats, cameras, and china). It required declarations about any foreign relations, by age, city, and location. Any errors or omissions in filling out these forms were liable to criminal penalties and fines.

When the full-time Jewish community administrators were given a deportation "order," the bidding started by first offering a list of names that would fill the scheduled transportation capacity according to the requisition while still leaving room for some exceptions. Within minutes after a deportation order was handed over to the Jewish official, usually two days before the time of arrival of the freight cars, everybody in the community knew what would be the likely outcome. That is when negotiations began, with desperate people looking for a loophole to disqualify someone in the family who would be a likely prospect. Since the required deportee quotas had to be met regardless of any exceptions, the time prior to the handing over of the final deportation list was the staging of traumatic and tragic episodes. The emotional relief that came from the news that a family was not on tomorrow's list was one of great satisfaction that was only clouded by the suppressed realization that this was only a deferral and not an indefinite release.

What nobody knew in the spring and summer of 1942 was that after the deportation of over 60,000 out of 80,000 Jews to annihilation camps in Poland the transports from Slovakia would suddenly stop, for reasons still disputed to this day. Those whose names did not make the transport lists were lucky enough to receive an extension on life for another two years.

My sister Ella owes her life to a freak accident in which her right hand was fractured when she fell. It was early in 1942, just as the transports were getting organized. At the age of seventeen she was most likely to be added to one of the early deportation lists that were labeled as relocation to "reeducation" camps to support the war effort. My father did not believe that story and saw to it that her hand was placed into an elaborate and heavy plaster cast that immobilized her entire arm. This disqualified her as an able-bodied worker. As soon as the last transport departed her cast was removed. Meanwhile, much of the muscle structure on her arm atrophied. She never recovered from that disability.

HOLOCAUST INFORMATICS

One of the contributions I made to the Holocaust Museum in Washington, DC was to identify the capabilities of punch-card accounting machines that were used by the German holocaust planners to schedule rail transportation of Jews efficiently. Although the entire railroad system in Eastern Europe was overloaded by military demands, the transportation of Jews was always given a priority and required careful logistics. I located, through my connections at the British Museum of Technology in London, an authentic German IBM machine manufactured in 1932 that was identical to the machine that was used for scheduling of transports to annihilation camps in the SS camp in Matthausen. This machine was still operating in Dresden in 1998.

The Holocaust Museum purchased and brought into a warehouse near Baltimore a tabulator, sorter, and keypunch machine sometime in 1991. I traveled to the Museum warehouse and positively identified the authenticity of this equipment, manufactured and maintained by the Deutsche Hollerith Gesellschaft (DEHOMAG), which was owned by IBM since the late 1920s. A retired IBM executive, who did not wish to be in any way identified, confirmed the support provided by DEHOMAG to the Nazi regime and provided me with the requisite technical documentation.

The circumstantial culpability of the IBM Corporation in these affairs is covered in a book for which I provided technical information.[1]

So far as I can tell, there was no "smoking gun" proof that the IBM personnel had actually scheduled deportations or knew what the machines were used for. Since I was responsible for managing an IBM tabulating installation from 1956 through 1959 in New York, I find such a plea specious. A claim that the ever-present IBM "systems engineers" were kept away from what was then a sophisticated machine accounting application is not credible. Alleging that the IBM experts did not know what was actually run at a major tabulating installation, at an SS location specializing in concentration camp management, is also not believable.

In 1990 I started working with a distinguished author and Holocaust historian, Dr. Sybil Milton, on a text that would accompany the exhibition of the tabulating equipment at the National Holocaust Museum in Washington, D.C. The purpose would be to devote a corner in the exhibit space to the "bureaucratization of the Holocaust." Its purpose would be to demonstrate that any dictator who had the power to employ the machinery of a sovereign state to systematically engineer murder could repeat such horrors. To my regret, I found that the Holocaust Museum in Washington, claiming a lack of space, gave this theme only minimal attention. The pain, anguish, and ghastly horrors of the atrocities now occupy almost all of the exhibit space.

I also find the museum was not much interested in giving much prominence to Jewish anti-Nazi resistance. The only way in which I can understand such a bias is by understanding the persistent inclination of most Jews to view themselves as helpless victims of acts committed by prejudiced anti-Semites. I tend to temper this view by seeing the Holocaust also as a deliberate design. The advent of genocide tendencies can be diagnosed in advance by listening to the rhetoric of the yet-emerging tyrants. In a number of cases, whether that was in Leningrad in 1919, Munich in 1928, Sarajevo in 1990 or Kampala in 1995, the advent of genocide could have been anticipated and countered by timely interventions before

---

1   Black, E., *IBM and the Holocaust*, Crown Publishers, New York, 2001.

a relatively small group of conspirators metastasizes into a position of absolute power.

HOLOCAUST MISINFORMATION

The placid submission of the Slovak Jews on the way to annihilation can also be explained by the skillful manipulation of information by the sophisticated murderers. The German and Slovak intentions were to cover up the killing. Simultaneously, the information conveyed by the Jewish leadership reflected the wishful thinking that the horrors awaiting the deported families would be somehow bearable. Over the years I discovered that those who are powerless especially dislike the bearers of bad news. The Jewish leadership was apprehensive that publicizing aggressively what was already known about the situation in Poland could lead to more violent measures that could be perversely invoked by the Germans to make them come true.

As Jewish families were loaded into freight cars, those who remained pleaded for letters to be written and sent upon safe arrival. The most frequent tranquilizer (and the message widely accepted by the Slovaks and the Slovak press) was the assertion that the entire relocation of the population was for the purpose of entering labor camps for "useful" work in support of the labor-short German war effort. Such propaganda was made believable by featuring in newspapers pictures of Jewish women sewing articles of clothing. The Slovaks delighted in a charade about the well-being of Jews by publishing stories about adequate housing. Receipts for food parcels were received without much delay. The guards who confiscated the food saw to that. None of these pretenses about the alleged living conditions in Poland could be verified because all independent sources of news were, for all practical purposes, shut out.

The transport of Jews to extermination camps in Poland was further confused by the decision of corrupt Slovak officials to create token labor camps in Slovakia. Because the treatment of Jews in such camps could not be hidden, the relatively benign treatment accorded to inmates served as a screen to hide the brutality and lethality of conditions elsewhere. The reason for keeping a small number of Jews in Slovakia, not more than

5,000 to 6,000 at any time, was to exploit their skills in carpentry and in metal trades as profitable slave labor. With cooperation from the remaining Jewish community, the deportations to the Slovak labor camps were always seen as the preferred option for anyone who could be classified as an able-bodied craftsman.

There were slave labor camps in Nováky, Vyhne, Sered, Žilina, Nitra, Láb, and Zohor. Conditions were survivable, though the inmates had to accept circumstances where they were subject to occasional physical abuse. This was particularly true in the period from 1941 to 1943 while the German war machine was winning the war. The abuses diminished after the German retreat from Stalingrad and many guards started hedging their bets.

The inmates lived in flimsy barracks, suffered from cold in winter, did not have enough food, and received only barely minimal medical care. As the transports to Poland were getting filled up much of the pleading and bargaining over whom to save concentrated on questions of who would be transported to one of the Slovak camps. Nováky had the "best" reputation because its post office functioned and it was relatively better managed as a self-organized community than the other locations.

The "White Card" Exemption

As the deportations proceeded, inexorably depleting the Jewish population in train-size increments, it became obvious to my father that the journey to Poland was a one-way trip to death. Whether my father knew about the news percolating from Osviecim about what was going on there was never clear to me. Whether anyone actually believed what the conveyors of the messages claimed is only a guess. What was told was so horrific that it was inconceivable. Such news was hard to accept while a smattering of letters praising conditions kept arriving.

For reasons I have never fully understood, while the deportations were still rolling in the middle of 1942, the president of the Slovak republic, a catholic priest by the name of Monsignor Tiso, instituted a special program then called a "Presidential Exemption." Its purpose was to exclude a very small and carefully selected number of Jews from deportation to camps. The exemption was certified by what was then called a white card. The frantic objective of every Jew who was still remaining in Slovakia was to figure out how to get a white card.

To become eligible for a Presidential Exemption called for an elaborate qualification process, such as checking on the reputation of the Jew in the community, evidence that one was already impoverished and that one complied with all conceivable laws and regulations. Most importantly, however, was the ability to claim that one was "economically essential" for the Slovak state. That had to be attested to by a politically prominent sponsor and endorsed by the local Hlinka Guards.

From his days on the district council my father became well acquainted while working with a Catholic priest, Monsignor Branecky, who was accorded great respect from the entire community as well as from the senior members of the Catholic church who in isolated cases exercised restraining influence on violence perpetrated by the Hlinka Guards. Branecky suggested that baptism would greatly improve our chances of getting a white card. If that would occur, he would personally intervene on behalf of my father with Msgr. Tiso.

Catholic baptism in those days, and even nowadays, was very difficult and time-consuming. My father then quickly reached an agreement with another close and highly respected Senior (equivalent to Bishop) of the Lutheran Church that an evangelical baptism would offer the most expeditious conversion to Christianity. Within three months after my bar mitzvah on January 24, 1942, my family started attending classes in catechism to prepare us for a formal baptism. That took place early in June 1942 while the deportations were still in progress.

Within weeks my father as well Mother, my sister and I received white card protection. It also applied, as a special act of charity, to Father's parents, which was a matter of uppermost concern to my father.

BAPTISM

The prospects of undergoing baptism while the deportations were taking place did not present me with too many anxieties. If that had to be done one had to do it. The alternatives were unacceptable even to contemplate. Whatever apprehensions my deeply religious mother would have had were brushed away in the rush to conform to all of the proper procedures and to fill out all the necessary forms. What made the entire affair easier was that my grandparents did not have to get baptized even though they would receive all of the benefits of my father's protection.

A few other Jews got baptized, too, if they had the time or sponsors to arrange it. In April and May of 1942 you would have signed your soul to the devil if all the devil was asking was a baptismal certificate. Besides, I did not have to wear the yellow star any more. We could not move back to our old home but came to view the entire baptism pragmatically as a way of saving our lives. Nevertheless, all of the other restrictive laws on movement, pleasures, subordination, marginal social status, and so forth still applied because even a baptized Jew was still legally defined as a Jew. All that mattered was the getting of a white card and not getting deported.

To become baptized an enormous amount of legal and procedural rigmarole had to be completed. We had to go to catechism school, study the Christian religion and its Lutheran variant (the Augsburg confession variety), understand what were the beliefs and dogmas and pass what was an easy examination on fine points of theology that separated the Lutherans from other evangelical churches.

In contrast with the Jewish religion, which allowed the widest possible interpretations of its doctrinal substance, which I never managed to comprehend, the heritage of the Lutherans was one of concentrating on the articles of faith, religious conduct and theological clarity. If you followed the prescribed procedures, attend church on Sundays, including the taking of sacraments, you were certified as having "done the right thing" and became qualified in the faith. Of course, everybody in the Lutheran community knew this was a charade. By being mostly loyal to the former Czechoslovak state as well as a minority surrounded by the aggressively assertive Catholic Church, the Lutherans viewed the acceptance of the newly minted parishioners as an act of Christian compassion and charity. I can characterize my two years in the Lutheran church as one of relative peace. Many people went out of their way to demonstrate genuine friendship. This happened amidst a world that ultimately closed this momentary respite that I still liken to the calm in the eye of a hurricane.

So far as I know, our conversion was never seen by anyone in our family as a betrayal of our heritage. My mother never talked about it. I was the only one who attended church with diligence because I found the organ music, psalms, and melodious hymns aesthetically very pleasing. The community singing was inspirational. The Sunday services had an appealing formal structure, which made going to church an interesting weekly experience because one could never guess what the choir or the organist was going to improvise next.

The Lutheran church in Trenčín was of the conservative Augsburg confession. This called for reading a different passage from the Gospels every week. The local pastor was partial to readings from the Old Testament and so I learned to understand more passages from the Hebrew Bible than I did formerly at the synagogue, where the text was read in ancient Hebrew, which I did not understand. Following the reading of the biblical passage came the Hymn, which was somehow related to the text that had been just cited. The hymns were melodic songs that originated from the works of famous baroque composers. The words were easy for the worshippers to follow and the tunes were simple enough for everyone to join in singing. After Hymn came the Oratorio, selected from the most tuneful works of some of the best composers, such as J.S. Bach, Monteverdi, or Handel. The service culminated in the Sermon from which I could readily discern cleverly worded anti-Nazi messages.

My young evangelical peers were friendly and accepted me without reservations to assist in organizing puppet theater performances staged every Sunday afternoon for little children. For a while I actually wrote some theater scripts, along with accompanying music that borrowed generously from Hebrew tunes. The entire group was highly musical and included a number of outstanding pianists and vocalists who delivered each Easter and Christmas a rousing Messiah chorus.

BACK TO SCHOOL

I was able to attend school because the headmaster was a friend of my father's and arranged that a special accommodation could be made for my attendance. Apparently, the school administrator found a loophole in finding an enrollment form that did not ask whether one was a Jew. Check marks on the registration forms listed only Christian faiths. I noted correctly that I was a Lutheran and in this way complied technically with the regulations while the cooperating officials stood by with a smile. You must understand such legalistic manipulations were taking place all the time in circumventing many of the lesser annoyances of Jewish existence. Exact technical compliance with bureaucratic demands is pervasive in that part of the world. It is well described in what is the most popular book ever written about such mentality, *Good Soldier Šwejk* by Karel Hasek. But, even Hasek could not imagine how conditions could evolve to totalitarian perfection when the Nazis or communists took over.

Another example of how formal compliance with legal minu-tiae could save lives is the case of the Kubičeks. They were transported to Žilina to a concentration camp from where weekly trains, each with about one thousand people, were dispatched to the Osviecim annihilation camp. Whenever a transport needed filling the required quota, a list was prepared by the Jewish administrators who then accompanied the Hlinka Guard who would herd the listed Jews into the freight cars.

The Jews in Žilina lived from week to week in petrified fear, never sure when their names would be called. Meanwhile, everybody was try-ing to find whatever avenue was available to get reclassified through any exemption that would place him or her into lower-priority rank on eligi-bility lists for deportations. When my father discovered that one of the ways for getting excused was American citizenship he took an affidavit in English signed by an American consul (I believe in Portugal) attest-ing that Mr. Andrew Kubiček declared his intent to travel to America. A combination of liberal bribes and a claim that this technically qualified the Kubičeks as "Americans" made it possible for the Kubičeks to return to Trenčín where they continued under my father's care until that was not possible anymore.

Meanwhile, the conditions at home were psychologically depressed as my parents, particularly my proud father, were subjected to an unceas-ing stream of humiliations. How my accomplished and proud parents could cope with that without transmitting this to family relations remains beyond my understanding. I must give much credit for this to my mother

END OF DEPORTATIONS

The deportations to Poland suddenly stopped early in September 1942. There are numerous speculations about the reasons why that happened, including a claim that it was an intervention from the highest levels in the Catholic Church after they were supplied with evidence that "resettlement" was actually genocide. The most frequently mentioned story tells of a very large bribe paid by the leadership of the Jewish community directly to Nazi officials. My best guess is that the Slovaks had already realized that there were no more economic gains to be realized after all of the Jewish properties had been successfully transferred into their hands. I also suspect, without evidence, that the actual cash payments from the Slovak Republic to the Germans for the transfer of the custody of the deported Jews left a well-documented trail of culpability for murder. The Slovaks, always mindful of possible legal consequences as well as needing clear titles to all confiscated property, must have given some thought to such possible consequences. Their history of quasi-legal plunder in 1860 and again in 1918 must have taught them lessons in how to make sure that plunder becomes legitimate property. Lastly, the battle of Stalingrad, the decisive military event of WWII, had already started in August of 1942. Father and I followed the failures of the Germans to advance every night, marking up a map whenever the Czechoslovak radio broadcasts from London reported the news. I also built an illegal crystal radio that was setup for tracking denials emanating from the local radio station. Repeated denials were always interpreted as a sign that all was not going well for the Germans in Russia. Whatever we knew must have been also unwelcome news to the Slovak Nazi collaborators.

The Slovak army that had until then advanced with the Germans to the foothills of the Caucasus Mountains had already started retreating in the summer of 1942. News was filtering in that some elements of the Slovak army had defected to the Soviets. As happened in all prior historical episodes (going back to the failed Turkish occupation of parts of Slovakia, including Trenčín) there must have been some thought given to protecting against any possible reprisals if political fortunes would turn. Besides, the remaining Jews in Slovakia were now employed in positions of considerable economic value to the Slovaks. They were worth more as intimidated cheap slave labor than as corpses that served no purpose except to satisfy Nazi ideology.

As we come to the close of the fist stage of the Slovak Holocaust, the following statistics sum up what was done:

The original Jewish population in the Slovak part of Czechoslovakia was 89,000, constituting approximately 4 percent of the total population.

An unaccounted-for portion of the population managed to flee. In addition, a part of Slovakia was ceded to Hungary prior to 1940 as part of the Munich Agreement. The best estimate is that this reduced the Jewish population at the time that the Slovak Nazi state came into existence to about 79,000.

The number of Slovak Jews deported to annihilation camps in Poland was 59,000. Because of careful accounting for payments from the Slovaks to the Germans, this number is well documented.

About 10,000 of the Slovak Jews were placed in forced labor camps, including a few in auxiliary battalions of the Slovak Army where the men were employed in hard labor in constructing military installations.

A small, but unaccounted-for, number of Jews disappeared altogether, mostly into villages where they assumed new identities and acquired false papers.

By September of 1942 this would then leave us with a remaining Jewish population in the Slovak State of fewer than 10,000, without property, stripped of all civil rights and subject to a long list of restrictions.

A small number of the remaining Jews received special privileges that varied according to local conditions. This included Jews of mixed marriages, holders of the "white card" presidential exemptions and some families that could claim citizenship (or some sort of a legal connection) to major Allied powers (such as the USA and Britain).

Here I have a semantic quibble. One finds frequent references in the Holocaust literature to Nazi "concentration camps." That is a misnomer. A concentration camp was a place where Jews were assembled for further transport to "annihilation camps." For instance, Žilina and Sered were used for herding Jews into a controlled space from where they could be transshipped to where organized murder could take place on a massive scale. Osviecim was an "annihilation camp," not a "concentration camp."

SURVIVOR STORIES

Of the 59,000 Slovak Jews deported in 1942, only a handful survived the war. The exact number of these survivors is unknown. I never gave much thought to that until it dawned on me that anyone who survived Osviecim for three years could have accomplished that only by becoming one of the Nazi-appointed lackeys who ran the camps, maintaining discipline among the inmates and managing the distribution of food. It is now a well-documented fact that only a very small SS cadre staffed the annihilation camps. By means of organized terror the "processing" of tens of thousands of inmates could be handled only through obedient intermediaries who were granted marginal survival privileges in return for their diligence in applying bestial practices. Although the Nazis preferred to use captive Russian prisoners and Polish criminals for such purposes they also had to depend on collaborating Jews to fill the ranks of enforcers.

A realization that all stories of survivors from the 1942 deportation era must be viewed with skepticism dawned on me during a flight to Tel-Aviv in 1979. I sat in the business class next to a Polish Jew from Frankfurt. As used to be the case with everyone after the war the first question following takeoff was "Where were you during the war?" This former inmate of Osviecim proceeded to tell me that he owned large real estate holdings in Frankfurt and had accumulated vast wealth rising from humble origins as a black market operator, and selling goods stolen from the American occupation army. When I inquired about his arrival date in Osviecim he said that it was early in 1942. He was proud describing how his fellows were able to organize for "self-help" preferential treatment and a better supply of food. He expressed pity for the 1944 arrivals from Slovakia and Hungary who had no "group cohesion" or a sense of "organization" and therefore ended up dying "like flies." When I pressed him about the nature of the "self-help," he refused to talk about it except to note that his name is listed as a major donor to several Holocaust memorials.

Recently I have picked up on many similar cases in which survivors of concentration camps refused to talk about their experiences. Several children and two grandchildren became interested in the history of the Holocaust to author essays for their college courses in European history. They could not get a word about those events out of their parents or grandparents. Since I do not classify myself as a "holocaust survivor" but as a talkative "resistance fighter," the students found it easy to interview me. My message is always that three-year inmates in Osviecim could achieve that only through deeds they would not wish to talk about.

The forms of denial about surviving the war are varied and often amusing. Every single senior German executive I met during my years as a global chief of computers for large US corporations (General Foods, Kraft, and Xerox) made sure that during the obligatory dinner parties for visiting executives, they sought me out, the sole Jew in the group, with what appeared to be a confessional that they had whiled away the war as low-level officers in German army antiaircraft defense forces.

ANOTHER OPTION FOR SLOVAKS?[2]

---

2   Source for this chapter is the *Holocaust Encyclopedia*, US Holocaust Museum.

In May 2003 I was asked to chair the Federal Holocaust Remembrance Day in Washington, DC. This is an annual event, and that year it was devoted to how the Bulgarians saved their Jewish citizens.

In 1934, Bulgaria had a population of more than six million people. In that year, Jews constituted 0.8 percent of the total population, or roughly 50,000 individuals. In terms of size and ratio of Jews, that was comparable to Slovakia.

In early March 1941, Bulgaria joined the Axis alliance and, in April 1941, participated in the German-led attack on Yugoslavia and Greece. In return, Bulgaria received most of Thrace from Greece, and Macedonia as well as parts of eastern Serbia from Yugoslavia. Although Bulgaria participated in the Balkan military campaign in support of Germany, they refused to enter the war against the Soviet Union in June 1941.

Beginning in July 1940, Bulgaria instituted anti-Jewish legislation, as dictated by the Germans. Jews were excluded from public service, discriminated against in their choice of places of residence, and restricted economically. Marriage between Jews and non-Jews was prohibited.

Germany-allied Bulgaria did not deport Jews. They did, however, deport non-Bulgarian Jews from the territories they had annexed from Yugoslavia and Greece. Jews of Bulgarian citizenship remained secure from deportation to German-held territory. Nevertheless, Bulgarian Jewish men between the ages of twenty and forty were drafted for forced labor, and in May 1943 the Bulgarian government announced the expulsion of 20,000 Jews from Sofia to the provinces. In the spring of 1943, the Bulgarian government made extensive plans to comply with the Nazi insistence that deportation of Bulgaria's Jews to Poland commence already. Protests from leading political and clerical leaders moved King Boris to cancel these deportation plans.

In 1945, the Jewish population of Bulgaria was still about 50,000, at its prewar level. Next to the rescue of Danish Jews, Bulgarian Jewry's escape from deportation and extermination represents the most significant exception of any Jewish population in Nazi-occupied Europe.

The saving of Bulgaria's Jewish community is one of the more remarkable stories of WW II and one of the least known. It happened in a country that was allied with Germany and the Axis powers. This is not to say that the Jews were not affected. Twice deportations of Jewish Bulgarian citizens were ordered, but in the end no Bulgarian Jew was sent to the death camps.

Several forces combined to save the Bulgarian Jewish community. The Bulgarian Eastern Orthodox church was especially honorable in this regard, probably more than any other church in Europe. They worked, both in public as well as privately, on behalf of their Jewish citizens. The efforts of Metropolitans Stefan and Kirgil were particularly noteworthy. The Bulgarian people and their historical attitude of religious tolerance were reflected in the fact that Jews, Christians, and Moslems had lived harmoniously together for centuries. In the northern part of the country, farmers threatened to lie down on the railway tracks, as did one of the leaders of the Bulgarian church.

THE BULGARIAN VS. SLOVAK SCORECARD

Bulgarian prewar Jewish citizen: 50,000; Postwar Jews: 50,000.

Slovak prewar Jewish citizen: 79,000; Postwar Jews: 6,400.

Bulgarian Army: Attacked Germans with Soviet Army support. Successful.

Slovak Army: Attacked Germans without Soviet Army support. Failure.

The Military

There were two principal resistance factions getting ready for victory even though each of them had splinter branches. There was resistance operated out of London by the legitimate Czechoslovak government in exile, headed by the elected President, Beneš. This group was relying on the Anglo-American political alliance to support the reconstitution of the prewar Czechoslovak republic.

There was also a Communist antifascist resistance organization run from Moscow acting as agents of the Comintern (the global Communist coordination agency). A changing cast of communist party functionaries who escaped to the Soviet Union in 1938 headed the Moscow operations.

The London as well as the Moscow groups started organizing for the postwar takeover of power as early as in 1942. The military goal set by the London-based command was to let the Soviet army sweep west without them destroying the towns and villages in Czechoslovakia. By 1944 the devastation of Russia, first by the retreating Soviets in 1941, then by the retreating Germans and then again by the advancing Soviets, made it clear that Czechoslovakia would end up as a wrecked countryside.

The Communist Party set the military goals for the Soviet army. The primary objective was to reconstitute Czechoslovakia as a Soviet state.

The Slovak army

The Slovak army continued to carry on many of the capabilities of what were well-organized and well-equipped Czechoslovak armed forces prior to the war. In 1944 the Slovak military constituted a formidable force for a country with a population of only four million. The active-service army was made up of two divisions with 37,000 men in readiness and with an additional 15,000 reserves callable on short notice. Only one of these divisions, placed in eastern Slovakia, was combat ready and well armed. They had at their disposal 300 heavy artillery pieces, 50 tanks, 42 airplanes, 100 antiaircraft guns supported by well-protected and well-stocked arsenals of ammunition, supplies and fuel. Almost all of these armaments were left over from the once powerful Czechoslovak army when it disintegrated in 1938.

A second division, placed in Western Slovakia, consisted mostly of troops for the logistics, transportation, medical and training support of the front-line contingent.

In 1939 the Slovak army participated in the attack by the Germans on Poland. They were the only Nazi ally participating in that action. In 1941 both divisions joined in the German attack on the Soviets. They were among the lead troops penetrating to the farthest line of German advances into the foothills of the Caucasus mountains. Slovak officers, many of whom were trained during the Czechoslovak republic, witnessed the destruction that took place on the eastern front. The idea that Slovakia would ultimately become a battleground was very much on their minds. From a career standpoint, the officer corps realized that they were risking a loss of their status, and possibly much worse in the eyes of the Soviets, who would treat them as criminals for the alleged atrocities while occupying Russia.

How to survive the end of the war was finally confronted early in 1944 when, under the guidance of the London-based Czechoslovak minister of defense in exile, military plans were drawn up to turn the well-armed Slovak divisions, now withdrawn from the Soviet front as potentially unreliable to the Germans war effort, to join the Allies as soon as the Soviets came near the Carpathian mountain passes. The idea was to attack the pass-defending Germans at the Dukla pass from the rear and then let the Soviets sweep through Slovakia for a relatively speedy occupation. Such a plan called for an organized armed uprising that would be supported by the Allied command, though without specific commitments because any actions on the eastern front were under the control of the Soviets. A few agents, officers from the Czechoslovak army in now in England, started arriving in Slovakia early in 1944 to establish liaison with their Slovak army officer counterparts.

It is not my purpose to dwell here about the muddled history of how the uprising was initiated, executed, bungled, and finally defeated. There is an enormous collection of books and documents that are contradictory in their interpretation of frequently unverifiable events. I must leave the untangling of the evidence to historians who will pick over whatever documentation is still left and will debate about what really happened for decades to come. The best I can do here is to tell the story the best way I know how from bits and scraps of conversations.

Preparing for the Uprising

In early 1944, my father, who indirectly controlled much of the food distribution business in the militarily critical Trenčín district, was party to moving a large quantity of food from regional depots to the village stores in the surrounding mountains. The excuse was that with the predicted severe winter weather the village stores needed bigger inventories because the roads would be getting muddy and gasoline was becoming scarce for too frequent resupply trips.

These moves coincided with actions initiated by cooperating government officials who started preparations for the coming uprising. By June of 1944 such a plot was a commonly whispered secret. Years later I found out that what Father was doing was a small part of much larger preparations involving the following:

Moving three months of food supply to the central region where the uprising would be concentrated.

Transferring money reserves as well as the gold reserves from the Slovak central bank to the central region. It is noteworthy that when the uprising collapsed at the end of October the Soviet command saw to it that the gold, and not the wounded, was evacuated on the last flights to Kiev.

Hiding 1.3 million liters of gasoline in mountain depots.

Relocating the entire army medical corps from the capital of Slovakia to the central region.

Such moves could not remain hidden from the ever-present agents of the Gestapo and Slovak Hlinka Guard informers. For the planners of the uprising to assume that a coup could come as a complete surprise was unrealistic. This error in planning assumptions and in a faulty intelligence ultimately unfolded into a series of erroneous decisions that ultimately doomed the uprising.

Perhaps the greatest fault in planning for the uprising came from the inability of the leadership to recognize that the original military plans did not conform to the conflicting and completely contradictory guidance received originally from London and then altered by Moscow.

Contradictory Political Guidance

The directives from London were simple. First, under no circumstances should the Slovak army provoke the German military into countermeasures until the Soviets could demonstrate that they were imminently ready to cross the Carpathian mountain passes from Poland and the Ukraine through Slovakia on the way to Budapest and Vienna. Only after the Soviet command would generate a signal to proceed with the uprising would the Slovak army have a chance of surviving. Second, since the Germans would not permit the Slovaks to take the initiative they would occupy Slovakia on the slightest provocation to protect their logistical hinterland. In such an event, the Slovak army would have to give up on the idea of holding any fixed positions. The insurgents would have to run for the hills from where they could conduct partizan warfare as was waged successfully in Yugoslavia.

The guidance from the political command in Kiev was ideological and invited the greatest damage and the most severe casualties to the Slovaks while diverting the largest number of German troops from fighting the Soviets. The objective here would be to liberate as much territory as was defensible and then to impose a Soviet regime in the occupied districts. The encircled Slovaks would have to hold until the Soviet army arrived. This recommendation was based on the premise that whatever the military outcome, any result would deliver political control to the Communists Party. This would make the Soviets the liberators and not the tainted Slovak army.

What was promoted from Kiev was in direct contradiction to the war plans (as recently revealed from the historical archives in Moscow) for the First Ukrainian Army commanded by Marshall Konev, the Second Ukrainian Army commanded by General Malinowski, and by the Fourth Ukrainian Army under General Petrov. Attack plans in the Soviet records showed that the Soviet army plans did not contemplate fighting in the mountainous regions of central Slovakia where the uprising was concentrated. The thrust of the advances of the Soviet armies aimed for the open plains where their motorized infantry and massed artillery barrages could win against the faltering German resistance.

24. Soviet Battle Lines, 8/19/44 to 12/31/44[1]

1   U.S. Military Academy, West Point, is the source of this map of the Soviet Southern command. See http://www.dean.usma.edu/history/web03/atlases/ ww2%20europe/ww2%20europe%20pages/ww2%20europe%20map%2030.htm. The heavy line shows the position as of 12/31/44 and confirms that the front lines remained stagnant since 8/19/1944 except where the Soviets exploited the switching of the Rumanian, Bulgarian and Hungarian armies from German to Allied allegiance (see the

It is noteworthy that the advice from Kiev reflected the guidance originally presented to Stalin at a conference in Moscow early in 1942 by the head of the Comintern, Georgi Dimitroff, who originally played the role as a provocateur in the famous Reichstag fire trials in 1933 that were instrumental in accelerating the accession of Hitler to power. In 1943 Stalin assigned the job of steering the resistance movements in Eastern Europe to his troubleshooter commissar, Nikita Khrushchev. Starting early in 1944, a headquarters was set up in Kiev with full authority to run partizan operations in occupied countries.

THE MILITARY VIEW

The military guidance from the Soviet command was strictly operational. Partizan warfare would start in June of 1944 with the drop of ten parachutist teams in mountainous spots near railroad lines that pass from the south to the north through the Carpathian mountain ranges. From a military standpoint that made sense because the High Tatra and the Low Tatra mountains are lined up in east-west directions with only three railroads crossing on the south-north track.

Early in 1944 the German command was still guessing whether the main line of the next Soviet attack would be coming through the heavily defended northern Polish plain or through the southern Danube basin. Since the battle of Kursk in 1943 the Soviet army had depended on massive tank armies and huge artillery barrages to punch through the German defenses regardless of losses. Therefore, the next attack would have to roll through the plains and not over the mountain range where defensible positions could be set up against any thrusts launched in the east-west direction.

As the Soviet military command saw it the purpose of any partizan actions would be primarily to interfere with the capacity of the Germans to shift troops and panzers northward or southward. The Slovaks and

---

shaded area). The thrust of the armies under Marshall Timoshenko were to advance along the Danube plain. Meanwhile the participants in the uprising were misled that the Soviet liberation was imminent.

whatever local partizans would rise to join them would serve the Soviet army best by diverting as many of the German resources from the front lines to protect their supply hinterland. Any disruptions in the rail traffic would reduce the reliance placed by the German commanders on the rapid redeployment of increasingly scarce military reserves.

From the Soviet army standpoint, partizans were dispensable manpower. Such an attitude was also reinforced by the NKVD (People's Commissariat for Internal Affairs reporting directly to Stalin) commissars who were spying on the army commanders and who viewed all partizans as operationally suspect and politically untrustworthy. Such bias became obvious when my partizan unit finally crossed the front lines in March 1945. The Slovaks were automatically transferred to the Czechoslovak army for security checking that would sort out any infiltrators. Our Russian partizans were handed over to the NKVD for deportation to unknown locations far away regardless of how these men had contributed to the war effort.

As the situation evolved the Soviet military point of view assumed a secondary priority, while the Soviet army partizan tactics were implemented with reasonable competence. That was done on a scale that did not make much of a difference to the outcome of the war in Slovakia, except that it saved my life.

The political objectives pursued by the partizan headquarters in Kiev ultimately prevailed. As the tragedy unfolded the Slovak army never followed the guidance from London even though that was their original intention. Especially after the uprising was precipitated by untimely events the Slovak army reverted to suicidal military tactics. As soon as civilians from Moscow and London tried to assert control over the military during the few weeks while there was a liberated territory, their conflicts worsened. Consequently, without any coherent leadership or a unifying strategy the uprising was doomed to failure.

Under such circumstances, the resistance fractured into small bands, each pursuing its own salvation. Operatives from the British intelligence, a thirty-two agent team from the American Office of Strategic Services, Jewish agents from Palestine, American pilots, German anti-Nazis, gypsies, Jews from labor camps, a contingent of airborne troops ferried from the Czechoslovak corps assembled during the war in Kazhakstan, turncoats from the Tiso regime trying to save their hide, liberated French soldiers, escaped prisoners of war, and scores of others ended up looking for ways how to survive.

PLANNING FOR THE UPRISING

A secret Slovak Revolutionary Council meeting, representing the major prewar political parties as well as the communists, took place late in May of 1944 in Western Slovakia. At this meeting the political representatives as well as a few key officers from the Slovak army agreed to trigger an uprising of the Slovak army so that the Soviets could cross the Carpathian mountain passes and liberate Slovakia quickly and with minimal civilian losses. A military operation to accomplish such a feat could be possible but only if such action would come as a surprise to the Germans. Full coordination with the timing and the deployment of the Soviet attack plans would be essential. The targets for the Soviet thrust across the Carpathians would have to be concentrated because there are only three mountain passes through these mountains through which a motorized army with tanks and supported with the usual Soviet artillery barrages could attack. The Slovaks were presumed to hold initially a tactical advantage in executing such a maneuver because at the time the plans were made there were no German combat troops in Slovakia. The entire plan hinged on securing trusted and rapid communications with the Soviet command.

The assumption that the Soviets would share with the Slovak army officers their battle plans was unrealistic. So far as the Soviets were concerned the Slovak officers, as allies of the Germans, were traitors. According to Stalin they would have to be executed. Therefore a jointly coordinated Slovak-Soviet military assault across the Carpathian mountains was an improbable scenario.

A member of the Slovak communist party underground *politburo*, Villiam Široky, attended an early May military planning meeting. Because any messages from a Slovak officer would be unacceptable, Široky was given the job to establish liaison with the Soviets since he claimed to be already in radio contact with the political command at the Kiev partizan

HQ. When June passed without progress from Široky making contact with the Soviets he alleged that his radio had malfunctioned and that he had to personally deliver the message to Khrushchev. The future chairman of the Soviet Politburo was at that time in charge of the political command of all partizan affairs. Khrushchev's job was to assure that Czechoslovakia would become a Soviet state after the end of the war. Such a directive did not include the job of cooperation with the Slovak army.

In due course, now desperate Slovak officers produced a hill-dodging military observation biplane that took Široky to Kiev where he promptly disappeared without a trace for several months. Relying on a Communist Party officer whose allegiance was to the political and not to the military was a terrible mistake. So far as I am concerned it was Široky who disabled the uprising even before it could start. For his service as a traitor to the Slovak uprising and as a faithful communist Villiam Široky was awarded with the post of prime minister of Czechoslovakia after the communists took over in 1948. It is noteworthy that Široky continued his job as a hatchet man by presiding over show trials and purges of prewar Communist Party idealists including party leaders who fought in the Slovak uprising and who could (or did) point to his role as the spoiler of anti-Nazi resistance.

The crossing by the Soviet heavy military forces would have to be timed and executed by Marshall Konev or General Malinowski within the framework of the overall war plans dictated by Stalin. That plan was to take all of Poland and most of Germany, including Berlin, through a frontal assault and in that process wipe out any residual Polish resistance who were not subservient to the communist controllers in Moscow. As was subsequently shown, the key assumption about the early and timely arrival of Soviet liberating troops was a figment. Early in 1944 it must have been clear to the military planners in London and in Moscow that the Soviet army high command would have no need to slog their way through the Carpathian Mountains to achieve their prime objective, which was the annihilation of the concentration of German forces now retreating to engage in the final defense of Berlin.

Fighting through the Dukla pass would take place to assure the penetration by the Soviet army into the Danube plain through Hungary in a southerly direction and certainly not to turn easterly to pass through the treacherous mountainous region of central Slovakia where the uprising would be staged. Besides, much of the burden, as well as casualties, of grinding through the well defended Dukla pass was put on the newly formed Czechoslovak corps formed from deserters from the Slovak army and patriots who had somehow survived the war by escaping in 1939 to Moscow.

I have to digress here for a moment and explain that in the summer of 1947 I hiked through one of the passes on the Carpathian Mountains. I was aghast when I surveyed the succession of bare hills surrounding the winding narrow road leading from Poland to Slovakia northeast of Žilina. It was readily apparent that the pass could be easily defended by a relatively small number of well-positioned gun emplacements. Only an infantry charging up the hill where there was no cover on the pastureland could take such positions. The hill would have to be taken in daylight for close support from artillery-happy Soviets. Their army did not fight at night, only the partizans did so. The local peasants told me about the enormous losses suffered by the Soviet infantry charging against dug-in positions in the last few days of the war at a time when occupying the mountain pass did not make military sense any more.

PREPARATIONS FOR DISASTER

It should have been also clear to the planners of the uprising that the Soviet political command would have no motivation to support a military coup carried out under the command of Slovak officers who were steered by policies emanating from London. Stalin would not wish to have a successful uprising won by an army that ideologically was largely beholden to the West, that had served under a fascist administration, that repeatedly displayed allegiance to the Catholic faith and that had successfully fought against the Soviets in prior years.

With the benefit of hindsight the Slovak uprising was doomed before it started. It made faulty assumptions about what the Germans could do. The Slovak officers, staging what ordinarily would be called a mutiny, did not have a fallback plan in case the Germans attacked with an overwhelming force, even though this possibility was given a high probability. The likely consequence of any uprising, without a joint battle plan with the Soviets, would surely meet the fate of the Polish Home Army in Warsaw that staged a similar coup and was wiped out. The planners did not benefit learning from the ghastly failure of the 1944 Warsaw uprising in which the Soviets halted their advance a few miles from where the Poles were getting murdered by the German SS counterinsurgency forces. Incidentally, after these units, the group Schill, finished off the Poles, they were immediately transported to Slovakia to perform a similar job.

The presumption of launching a surprise attack on the German troops also overlooked the generally known intelligence that the entire conspiracy was monitored by German intelligence all along. Despite all of these fatal flaws, the planning to carry out the original intention of staging a defection of the Slovak troops continued as the summer progressed. Without the planners having much control over the events, the much-anticipated uprising started prematurely on August 28, 1944.

Whether the uprising by the Slovak army was set up for failure by means of a clever communist-inspired conspiracy or by misfortune does not matter and will never be known with certainty. There is no proof that would support a conspiracy theory except that the events that unleashed the sequence leading to the ultimate disaster were triggered by a Russian commando group operating under Soviet control despite agreements to avoid precipitating a premature attack on any German commands. So far as I am concerned a communist conspiracy could be a plausible explanation that connects the sequence of events that led to the demise of the uprising. There are also memoirs that point to the many faults in how the Slovak command was organized, including instances of hard-to-believe incompetence. When all of that is combined with muddled execution of military actions the inexorable disaster was preordained.

TRIGGERING THE UPRISING

On the night of the 25th of August, one of the parachuted Russian commando squads boarded an already stopped passenger train that was returning from Bucharest to Berlin at a minor railroad station where you put water into the tenders for the resupply of a steam locomotive for passage over the Carpathian Mountains. It was largely a Russian team who had arrived in Slovakia a month before. As compared with the now desolate countryside in the newly liberated Soviet lands, the Russians found Slovakia a land of undreamt prosperity with a practically unlimited supply of food, alcohol, clothing and enthusiastic women. My best guess is that they went after the train with the intent to rob it. They were crazy about acquiring watches and anything made of gold. To the surprise of the Russians they found that the sleeping cars were full of German general staff officers and their deputies who were returning from a meeting in Bucharest to plan defenses of the southern-tier countries against the incipient Soviet army onslaught. What happened after that, and what was the sequence of events and what was the role of the Slovak soldiers in the executions of the German officers is still disputed matter.

The Russian commandos, following agreed rules between the Slovaks and the partizans, handed over the German officers to the Slovak army who then escorted them to the Slovak army quarters nearby. The Germans were assured that they would receive safe sleeping quarters as well as protection against possible harm from the "bandits" because proceeding further on the train would be too dangerous. The Germans, still well armed, did not have much of a choice and left the railroad station to spend the night at the Slovak quarters. In the morning, as is customary in military quarters, everyone lined up on the parade grounds with fully loaded arms.

The local Slovak commander was under strict orders from Lieutenant Colonel Golian, now the titular head of the planned uprising, to make sure that no harm would come to any captured German because that would invite countermeasures before anyone was ready. Whether some trigger-happy Slovak or a hidden Russian fired the first shot on the parade grounds, or, as has been often proposed, some provocateur fired from a building nearby, will never be known. Suffice it to say that the Germans started defending themselves and the Slovak machine guns mowed them down.[2]

---

2   Major conflagrations, even without a strategic purpose, can be often be trig-

What Happened?

The events surrounding the massacre of the German officers that prematurely triggered the uprising have remained a mystery to this date so far as I know it. Historians of the uprising have offered completely different versions of what happened. My own speculation reflects my experiences as a member of a small Soviet commando squad that was organized and controlled in identical ways as the one that stopped the train with the German officers. We were under strict orders to avoid engagement with the Germans or their support troops because our mission was to disrupt railroad traffic and not to conduct combat that would result in reprisals against the civilian population and give an incentive to hunt us down. Our job was to finish what we were supposed to do and then disappear without casualties, which we could not carry anyway. We went out of our way to avoid a firefight unless that was forced on us.

The fact that the partizan unit that extracted the German officers from the train did not shoot them on the spot was consistent with our own orders. Handing the Germans over to the regular Slovak army would also follow the orders to the parachuted Soviet squads to concentrate on setting up bases for such time as when the partizan command in Kiev would dictate more aggressive actions against German transportation links. That would take place only when coordinated with the Soviet offensive that was scheduled to start later in the fall. With such an understanding as well as with the now vague recollection of fireside chatter among the Russian partizans that the killing of the Germans by the Slovaks spoiled their comfortable set up, I am led to conclude that the trigger event for the uprising was badly mistimed accidentally. It was a stupid mistake rather than some premeditated conspiracy, which of course describes much that happens in any war.

When it comes to understanding military and political matters I follow the Machiavelli rule, "Do not look for a conspiracy when incompe-

---

gered by what otherwise would be only unfortunate incidents. The historian Barbara Tuchman, in her masterly book *The Guns of August*, described how World War I started even though nobody intended it to do so at that time.

tence can explain it all." It is also noteworthy that not more than about fifty Soviet partizans parachuted into Slovakia as ten geographically separated teams. These men came from Byelorussian units that had been disbanded by the NKVD who never trusted a partizan but considered them still suitable to take on yet another suicidal mission. These were desperate men, half starved and poorly clothed when they landed. Suddenly they arrived in a country where they were welcome as liberators by the Slovak villagers. These guys had little incentive to stir up trouble with the Germans that would disrupt this cozy setup.

German Countermeasures

Immediately after the news of the massacre leaked out, the Gestapo proceeded to implement their preplanned countermeasures that called for the disarming of the Slovak army to prevent it from participating in an uprising. The Germans must have concluded that the execution of the German officers was the signal for the uprising to commence. Proceeding with punitive reprisals against the killers of high-ranking German officers was also a sufficiently good reason to do something drastic.

The undermanned Gestapo and the limited number of SS-police troops were not able to disarm most of the Slovak army in the western part of Slovakia with headquarters in Trenčín. The lower-ranking officer corps had been preparing for a mutiny anyway to join the winning side in the war and to salvage their careers. In the resulting small-scale scuffles the Nazis were overwhelmed. Meanwhile a radio station slipped under the control of a radical faction of the civilians in Banska Bystrica and started broadcasting that the uprising had started.

The original conspirators who had been planning the uprising for almost a year then proceeded with the execution of plans that had been conceived in London almost a year earlier. It was Lieutenant Colonel Golian who finally issued the agreed signal to commence with the uprising in the morning of August 29 of 1944. Subsequent political developments quickly took the control of events out of the hands of the Slovak military and transferred it to the communist leadership. After that the Soviets were in control politically though the responsibility, and the eventual blame, for the execution of all military actions was placed on a small number of Slovak officers.

THE ROOT OF FAILURE

The original plans depended primarily on the combat-ready division of 15,000 located in the eastern part of Slovakia to join the uprising. They were adequately equipped with heavy arms to take and hold the Dukla pass until the Soviets would join them. The commander of the eastern army, General August Malar, demanded that the insurgency headquarters in Banska Bystrica, run by lower-ranking staff officers, prove that the Slovak army would be coordinated with the Soviet moves. In the absence of a message that such joint action would be taking place, Malar refused to issue orders to his troops while waiting to hear the good news that one could proceed as planned. The communication link between Malar and the Soviet command was never established. The uprising HQ in Banska Bystrica had nothing to report while still scrambling for a commitment from the Russians. While Malar hesitated, a relatively small contingent of German troops arrived from reserves in Poland and disarmed Malar's battle-hardened soldiers without firing a shot. For all practical purposes any prospects of a military success of the uprising were now gone.

The unfolding of the uprising in the western part of Slovakia showed mixed results. Individual units of the Slovak army defected from their local garrisons in small units and not under a unified command. These were reserve troops without major combat experience or arms capable of resisting motorized German infantry supported by panzers and with close air support. In the absence of a clear organization for command, about half of the soldiers returned home and changed into civilian clothing. Some of their commanders remained loyal to the Tiso regime, such as the Nitra garrison of 2,000 soldiers, who joined the SS in attacking uniformed Slovak army units that decided to support Golian who had now been promoted to full general rank by the London government.

The fact that a general reporting to the London government now headed the Slovak uprising made it certain that the Soviets would never trust any Slovak military commander even when wearing Czechoslovak shoulder patches. Golian, formerly a staff officer without field combat experience would also become unacceptable to the communist civilians who took over key government positions. The communists who arrived from their Moscow exile concentrated on asserting control over the government in the liberated territories instead of focusing on the organization for survivable defenses.

The premature precipitation of the Slovak uprising was started by what may have been an isolated and possibly an unpremeditated act. However, the unintended consequences of the assassination of the German officers by a handful of soldiers ignited events that within a few days enveloped over 100,000 combatants and perhaps as many as a million civilians. Students of history and politics should find in the rapid unfolding of these events a source of insights on how many small errors can accumulate to escalate into a combination of mistakes that will yield unexpected outcomes. Perhaps the principal reason why the events took uncontrollable turns was the absence of communications. The stakeholders in the uprising, the London exile government, the Moscow communist conspirators, the Soviet partizan command in Kiev, the Soviet military planners and at least two different Slovak army factions, did not and could not communicate rapidly because they were technically not equipped to do so.

Even if they had been able to set up the appropriate communications links there was not much of a chance that effective cooperation would take place anyway. The various actors in this tragedy pursued divergent political and military objectives even though they were unified in fighting the Nazis. The end of the war was nearing and the contest for assuming postwar powers had already begun, even though reality dictated the need to focus on the approaching failure. When the allied emissaries from the British Special Operations Executive (SOE) as well as the American OSS landed sometime in mid-September for liaison and observation purposes all they could do was to stand by and watch from their Banska Bystrica quarters how an already doomed military adventure spiraled toward failure.

Incidentally, almost all of the SOE and the large OSS contingent, headed by an inexperienced US Navy officer, were killed by the SS after the failure of the uprising.

Warfare Unfolds Into a Family Tragedy

To minimize the damage, the local Gestapo and collaborators proceeded with the execution of their own plans. During the night of August 28 they raided the homes of the key suspects in towns where there were army bases, with the divisional HQ in Trenčín getting highest priority. My father was taken among the first prisoners and was severely beaten. The man in charge of the abduction was a young Slovak by the name of Kraus who had recently joined a Nazi auxiliary that consisted of men claiming to be of German origin. Kraus was an educated son of a prominent local architect who knew my father well. When armed violence was unleashed by the uprising, the response by the pro-Nazi faithful was to apply indiscriminately a level of brutality that would be used for "bandits" and "terrorists," with Jews singled out for exceptional cruelty.

The Lesson for a Lifetime

The sequence that started in 1938 with the deprivation of civil rights and the confiscation of property of my father until he was beaten and carted off to an extermination camp in September of 1944 has imparted a deep imprint on my consciousness forever. It gave me an insight into how thin is the veneer that overlays what is claimed as human civilization. It nurtured a path of inquiry to comprehend the dynamics of the progress that has been made from primitive savagery to the current stages of evolution. After witnessing the disintegration of the social fabric in previously benign Slovakia I developed a lifetime compulsion to understand what holds any society from tearing itself asunder whenever the envelope of civility is removed.

After many years of searching, and largely influenced by the good fortune of living in peace in America, I came to define human freedom as the capacity of a community to offer predictable expectations that justice will prevail at all times, for everyone. For freedom to exist, one must follow the path that has been set forth by the milestone that has defined for me as the foundation on which one must sustain a humane civilization. That is the Ten Commandments, which is a heritage passed from the Jews to all mankind that no persecution can expunge.

The crimes against my family started with a disregard of their rights as citizens that were accorded to all other Slovaks. Such injustice was further compounded by a sequence of laws that progressively denied their existence as human beings. Finally, the injustice was culminated by violations, even by the highly religious Slovaks, of God's laws. Whereas injustice could be disguised before the Slovak population by the legalistic charades from 1938 through 1942, when killing was subcontracted to the German annihilation factories, the Slovak government and the Hlinka Guards could not wash their hands any more of being guilt-free. When the time came to get rid of Jews in 1944, all appearances of legality could be dispensed within everybody's sights. It is the horror of wars that they break down the rules that sustain a civil order and give leeway to a regression to conditions when life was primitive and brutal.

The Situation

By the second week in September of 1944, probing skirmishes took place using undermanned counterinsurgency SS police. The Germans started with raids on a few enclaves where army deserters were located in western Slovakia. In most cases the Germans were beaten when they ran into fixed defense positions that the Slovak army was trained for. Particularly noteworthy here was the stand of French army prisoners of war who somehow landed in Slovakia at the start of the uprising when a freight train transporting them was intercepted by partizans. With armories open the prisoners quickly managed to organize into a highly motivated fighting force. They demolished a German unit in a narrow mountain pass with only light arms. The German counterinsurgency troops quickly figured out that heavier attack forces were needed to root out an army that was starting to dig into fixed positions. Much of the early days in September were then spent by the SS in applying terror where hardly anyone was in a position to shoot at them.

It is during this period that a large number of executions took place, which included mostly Jews who were seeking refuge wherever the uprising occupied a territory. Immediately after the start of the uprising the geography covered by the reincarnated Czechoslovak state was about 100 by 250 miles. That area started shrinking after the initial probing attacks by German forces. The Slovak army, trained for conventional warfare, kept withdrawing into more defensible mountainous districts centered on the town of Banska Bystrica. With prospects of connecting with the Soviets advancing over the Carpathian Mountains receding, the morale of the Slovak troops kept sinking. Whenever the German launched an attack the defenders fled, except in a few instances when they succeeded to slow down the enemy's advances for a few days. It was just a matter of time before the German armor, supported by dive-bombers, would close in on the steadily shrinking territory and drive the remaining forces to flee into the mountains.

By mid-October, elite SS troops, including the combat division that had just eliminated the Polish Home Army in the second Warsaw uprising, started arriving in Slovakia. Using good intelligence the Germans maneuvered into position for a coordinated attack on the center of the liberated. The attack was concentrated on the forces that deployed around Banska Bystrica where the military units, using conventional warfare tactics, had assembled to defend what was now designated as "liberated Czechoslovakia."

With the political and military forces of the uprising all concentrated in only one location, a fatal flaw in all partizan operations, the primary objective for the German military was to decapitate the central command. The secondary objective was to deny the uprising its only airfield, which had provided the only means for connecting with the Allies. The grass-covered regional airfield (Tri Duby) was located near Banska Bystrica and had to be eliminated as a potential landing for Soviet airborne reinforcements. Landings of six American B-17 bombers accompanied by P-47 fighter escorts early in October highlighted the strategic importance of the Tri Duby airfield.

Without coordinated command and control capabilities, with conflicting (or nonexistent) strategic guidance, without tank armor, in the absence of air cover and with political squabbling between the communists and the London leadership sustaining a large liberated territory 300 kilometers behind the front lines was not feasible. By October 28, 1944 the last traces of "liberated Czechoslovakia" were wiped out. Slovak army soldiers melted away into their native villages. Those who were caught were shipped to camps in Germany where they were treated as "bandits" and not prisoners of war. With the exception of partizans now completely under Soviet command and a few remnants of the Czechoslovak resistance the uprising was finished.

THE COLLAPSE OF THE UPRISING

Five weeks after the last remaining territory of liberated Czechoslovakia fell my partizan squad had to pass over a section of the road (north of Donovaly where most of the Slovak army troops fled) over which the Slovak soldiers' retreat had taken place. Although the ground was already snow covered, the chaos and the casualties among the withdrawing troops were evident. We passed piles of helmets, backpacks, cracked-open ammunition cases, burned-out trucks, abandoned antiaircraft guns and bullet-riddled ambulances. Though we were warned about unexploded ordnance, we managed to pick up many frozen uniforms which came in handy because our own garments were in a deplorable condition and insufficient to protect us against the cold. No shoes or boots could be found. It was apparent that the retreating Slovak soldiers were getting rid of all of their military gear. They must have changed into civilian clothing and started walking back home.

FIGHTING WAS THE ONLY OPTION

The Jewish partizans had no place to go. Consequently the ratio of Jews to all others remaining in combat service grew after the end of October. The survival rate of the non-Jewish partizans, mostly ex-soldiers plus the highly experienced Russians, was better than that of the Jewish partizans. The Jews who had no prior military training, but the determination never to be captured, took heavier casualties. Even then, of the about 2,000 Jews, including 200 women, who joined the partizans, about 500 are accounted for as killed. That meant that 75 percent of the people who fought survived. Nevertheless, our odds of survival were certainly better than those who were captured or deported to camps.

Such numerical comparisons cannot prove that a guerrilla fighter has a greater than what I estimate as a ten-times-better survival chance than somebody who took their chances with the genocidal enemy. In guerrilla warfare experience, attitude and capabilities are more important than just the numerical odds that are in favor of the guerrillas anyway. Most of those deported to annihilation camps were people to whom the concept of guerrilla fighting was alien. They were people with no prior experience in how to hide and survive in a hostile countryside. They never even tried to learn how to use weapons. Even when arms became widely available during the early stages of the uprising most of the Jews were looking for places to hide rather than take up arms.

The fear that had been instilled into Jews during the prior five years deterred them from taking any actions that would have involved doing anything that could be considered illegal. The Jewish religious leadership who followed the "learn how to submit" traditions promoted much of this sentiment. Thus most of the adult Jews, even combat-capable men, did not prepare themselves to consider resistance as a viable survival choice.

I am sure that many readers will find my judgment about the lack of a commitment to fight insensitive to the circumstances and to the prevailing cultural biases of the Jewish community in Slovakia. My views in this regard are influenced by my exposure to American and Israeli ways of thinking where the commitment to armed defense is shared by much of the population, with the exception of the extremely religious Jews. However, after the arrival of two Jews who escaped from the Oswiecim annihilation camp early in 1944 and the reported details about conditions, there was no possible justification for further rationalization about what would happen when the Germans would finally take over control.

So far as I know none of the rabbis who debriefed the escapees and who had compiled comprehensive reports about genocide for transmission to the Allies, had set into motion a campaign to encourage Jews to protect themselves by commencing immediately a dispersal into villages, sheds or hideouts. Places that were far away from urban centers, military bases, potential defense strong points or major transportation hubs would offer a more sustainable refuge during the months (or weeks) while the terminal phase of the war would come to pass. That did not happen. With minor exceptions Jews continued to maintain a sense of what they then considered as normalcy, as deprived as it was. As the end of the war approached the Jews were concentrated in urban centers where they would be most vulnerable to instant capture. Missing in the prevailing thinking was a view of the impending doom as seen in military terms. To the rabbis, such ideas would be alien and counter to the experiences acquired during centuries of persecution, except that now it was not persecution but prospects of almost certain death as the retreating Germans would surely do everything to wipe out the remaining traces of European Jewry.

I am convinced that the survival rate of the more than 20,000 Slovak Jews, who were still around at the beginning of the uprising would have been better if they had been willing to gain the necessary experience, capabilities and a more active attitude to choose dispersal and, if necessary, resistance when it was the only remaining choice. In the absence of inspired leadership and without a spirit to die as a free people rather than be slaughtered as passive victims, most of the Jews never considered the option of choosing armed survival in mountain refuges as a realistic choice.

If there is one universal lesson from the Slovak uprising it is this: Those who will inflict genocide will not be dissuaded by diplomacy or appeals, or bribes. Until justice prevails in the world, and that is not likely to happen in this generation or the next one, the potential victims have no other choice than to be prepared to resist and to do that competently. I am proud to have participated in the Slovak uprising. It convinced me that resistance to evil is a cost we all must be always be willing to incur as the price of freedom.

After the Collapse of the Uprising

The main German armed forces withdrew from Slovakia immediately after the elimination of the liberated area and returned to the main battleground that was now shaping in the Polish plain. They left police troops, composed mainly of ex-Soviet prisoners of war of Ukrainian, Lithuanian and Latvian descent who had been commissioned by the SS to act as executioners. These troops were highly skilled in anti-insurgency warfare. One of these units had just finished murdering thousands of Poles who capitulated after the failure of the Warsaw uprising. The SS-police troops were brutally efficient and used raiding tactics that were indistinguishable from the combat methods used by Soviet partizans. Their favorite ruse was to put on clothing that made them look like they were Soviet partizans. In one case they walked into partizan encampments talking loudly in Russian and then machine-gunning the occupants. Using such pretense they often managed to flush out Jews or civilians who were hiding and revealed themselves seeking assistance. The duped victims were tortured to betray others and then murdered on the spot.

After the demise of the Slovak uprising, the SS took 19,000 military prisoners, of whom 5,000 were Jews. The Hlinka Guards then devoted their efforts to capturing the remaining Jews, with an estimate that 13,500 more were deported. No more than 5,000 Slovakian Jews remained in the country either as partizans, in hiding or with false identities.

RUMANIANS, BULGARIANS AND HUNGARIANS

The ineffective and subsequently defeated Slovak uprising must be also understood in the context of actions taken by other German military allies.

On August 25th, 1944, the Rumanian government declared war on Germany. Its army joined the Soviets in the drive west and ended up occupying parts of Slovakia. The Rumanian switch took place smoothly and with hardly any retaliation from the Germans. The civilian population did not suffer losses from getting situated in battlefields.

On September 8th Bulgaria switched sides and declared war on Germany. The Bulgarians joined the Soviets and occupied the entire country, without destruction of town and villages. This rapidly and well-executed reversal in allegiance avoided civilian casualties and saved the lives of every Jew.

On October 15th Hungary announced the end of hostilities against the Allies. On October 18th the Hungarian army joined the Soviets in attacking German positions. Lives and property were saved.

The rapid turning of armies from being supporters to becoming attackers of the German military is critically important in making a judgment about the bungled Slovak uprising. In my view, it took exceptional incompetence to create conditions that resulted in a murderous transition to liberation.

The actions of Slovaks must be compared with those taken by the Rumanians, Bulgarians and, Hungarians. In each case the switching from the losing side to the winning side took place almost simultaneously with the defection of the Slovak army. It is probable that my family could have been saved had it not been for the arrogant disregard of the military and political realities by the Slovak leadership, who tried to follow contradictory and conflicting ideas, without accountability for what would be the consequences.

A Postscript

Postscript

I left Trenčín early in February, 1948 for Paris and then for London. Arrived in New York on October 15, 1948 as an immigrant, with $26 in my pocket. I started working immediately, selling socks at the Gertz department store in Jamaica, New York.

Graduated from the tuition-free Cooper Union in New York, with an engineering degree, in 1953. Worked my way through M.I.T., ending in 1955 with a master's degree in industrial management.

Have been married to Mona since 1954. Our marriage produced Vera (Johns Hopkins), Andrew (Carnegie-Mellon), Steven (M.I.T.) and the much admired and beloved Eric (Harvard, died in 1984). There are six grandchildren, at present.

I started working with computers in 1954, which led to positions with progressively rising responsibilities for the management of information technologies as the chief information executive for General Foods, Kraft, Xerox, Department of Defense, and NASA (1962 to 2003).

At present I hold the position of Distinguished Professor of Information Sciences, George Mason School of Information Technology and Engineering, following an academic appointment as adjunct professor at the US Military Academy at West Point.

In 1993 I received the Defense Medal for Distinguished Public Service, the Defense Department's highest civilian recognition. In 2002 I was honored as recipient of the NASA Exceptional Service Medal. As long as I can I will continue serving as a grateful citizen of the United States of America for giving me an opportunity to live in peace.

Over the years I have published over 250 articles and five books on information management and information worker productivity.

The text about the Trenčín years has been in a scattered draft form for the past fifteen years. The time has now finally come to assemble the text and publish it before my memories start fading.

For the past sixty-five years I have succeeded in diverting my thoughts from the past and to concentrate entirely on building for the future. In my declining years I decided to commit my remembrances of past events to writing. Here is a story where sometime, somewhere, somebody may discover insights into how to cope with hardships that will continue to be inflicted on generations to come as long as justice and freedom remain only a temporary blessing.